From **darkness**
into the
light

MARINO RESTREPO

Note to the Reader:
Throughout the book, the words "man", "men", "mankind", "he", "his", "himself", "brothers", "sons", are denoted as being all-inclusive, respecting both genders.

Published by eBookIt.com

ISBN 978-1-4566-3495-7

www.marinorestrepo.com

In homage to the Catholic Church

and to the mission of
Pilgrims Of Love

Contents

Preface

It is quite satisfying for me to write a prologue to this testimony, which has been written as a sincere and audacious confession, full of humility and love for the truth. These traits are evident very negatively in the first part of the book and quite positively in the second part. It is a resurrection that would not have happened without dying first.

Three references can lead the reader to meditate about the Love of God that keeps human hearts alive today. The references — taken from the apostle Peter, St. Augustine and St. John of the Cross — are twenty, sixteen and five centuries removed from us.

Saint Paul says:

"...as all have sinned and have the need of the glory of God. They are justified freely by his grace through the redemption which is in Christ Jesus, whom God has set forth as a propitiation by his blood through faith, to manifest his justice, God in his patience remitting former sins; to manifest his justice at the present time, so that he himself is just, and makes just him who has faith in Jesus".

1 Romans 3: 23-26

Saint Augustine says:

"You would have died for eternity, unless he had been born in time. You would never be set free from the stain of sin, unless he had taken to himself the likeness of the flesh of sin. You would have been in the grip of everlasting misery, had it not been for the occurrence of this great mercy. You would not have come back to life, unless he had adjusted himself to your death. You would have faded away, if he had not come to the rescue. You would have perished, if he had not come. Let us celebrate with joy that our salvation and redemption have come".

Sermons of St. Augustine, Bishop
Sermon 185 PL 38

Saint John of the Cross says:

"Truly, this soul is lost to everything else but love, its life being dedicated to nothing but love. Therefore, active life and other external actions weaken on account of that 'one single thing' that her Beloved deemed 'necessary': the presence and continuous practice of God's love".

St. John of the Cross.
The Spiritual Canticle, Stanza 8.
Translation of commentaries nn 1-3,
pp. 934-935, Edic. BAC, 1960

At the age of 47, God's light entered into Marino's brilliant artistic career and showed him his own darkness and that of other human beings who had violently deprived him of his physical freedom.

Paradoxically, that loss turned into true spiritual freedom due to the merciful gift Marino received from Jesus Christ. The radical change that the Lord caused in him gave him understanding of his own life and turned it into a joyful apostolic mission.

Marino's actions have been notably supported by divine inspiration ever since. The warmth, advice and spirit of the Church have provided him with great security and doctrinal vision. In all his lectures, he is always ready to give advice to enthusiastic priests, willing to sacrifice himself to do God's will in his own life and that of others who, moved by his testimony, have joined the regeneration movement of thousands of people in different countries.

I am grateful to Marino for his friendship and his brave example.

Rafael Vall-Serra, S.J.
Director of ECOM
(Spanish acronym for 'Gospel Communicated')
Bogotá, April 2003

Introduction

This past decade has witnessed the publication of many works of faith, testimonies, of personal experiences that diverse men and women have written to share, the mysteries of grace, love, forgiveness and one of these is this present testimony of the conversion and the faith of Marino Restrepo.

Marino was born in the highlands of Columbia. At the age of 19 he moved to Germany, where he married and had two sons and studied the arts. He soon succumbed to the allure of Hollywood and was immersed in everything that Hollywood had to offer — success, money, pleasure, beautiful women and the new age. His was the story of a prodigal son. In 1997, he returned for a visit to his native homeland and soon after was caught up in the drama of being taken hostage by the rebels and kept prisoner for 6 months in caves and jungles, expecting death at any moment.

Here, he experienced the love of Jesus Christ that transformed his life, and washed away his sins, and that called Marino to a life of witness to the power of faith and the love of Christ. His was not only the story of his personal conversion; the Lord called him to proclaim his Gospel of Mercy which he has done in many countries around the world. With the story of a lost faith rediscovered and the story of the Father's loving embrace that washes away his sins with his Father's tears and the blood of his Son, it has become as his lyre-trumpet of the Holy Spirit who continues to witness the saving message of the Gospel of Christ through the world of today.

I commend and recommend this story of faith and the love of Christ to everyone.

15th day of August 2005.
Bishop Roman Danylak.
Titular Bishop of Nyssa.

Testimony

To speak of an encounter with God means penetrating the most personal side of human beings; it means talking of their Creator, provided that they believe such a Creator exists. For those who do not share this belief, it means speaking of an all-embracing fantasy they call God. In any case, one is faced with the difficulty of communicating either a deeply felt testimony of an encounter with that Creator, or an illusive one, in the case of non-believers.

There are two main reasons for a human being to publicly confess an encounter with God: the first one is the need to share with others a supernatural experience that cannot be kept naturally; the second one is the divine inspiration to reveal that God-given encounter which forces the person to communicate — in the form of a message — all the teachings that God has infused in his spirit. It could be said that if God has chosen someone to have a personal encounter with him, the onus is on that individual to communicate and attest to such an encounter for the benefit of souls.

Among the inscrutable mysteries of our Creator are the thousands of personal encounters with His creatures. Innumerable passages of the Scripture refer to them. The meaning and purpose of the messages are closely related to that moment in time when the revelation takes place, as well as to the human instrument where that grace is deposited. Some private revelations have been given to nuns or monks, to help them be a light in their monasteries and communities, as well as a spiritual inspiration to those around them. Often these revelations only come to light many years after they have taken place. When the purpose of a revelation is to reach a large number of souls, the messenger feels this urgency and receives the necessary gifts to complete his mission.

The story you will read fits into the latter description. Everything I received in my encounter with the Lord is to be communicated to all those chosen by him to receive this message.

The most incredible thing about the testimony you are about to read is that it is not new at all; it does not say anything that has not already been revealed or written. However, in obedience to our Lord, I will communicate it, being aware that the truth can be expressed in an infinite number of ways and even though being the same truth, it seems to renew itself in each creature. If the truth tired us, we could not bear to see the same old sun or moon everyday. But these always-shining stars look like a new sun and moon to us every day.

The encounter I will narrate occurred during the time of my kidnapping that began on December 25, 1997 in Colombia, South America. My intent in referring to this event is to share with the reader the mystical experience that motivated this book.

The political situation of Colombia and the reasons prompting insurgent groups to commit such crimes have no bearing on the story. Thus, everything conveyed about Colombia and these criminals is strictly related to my spiritual experience. The Lord's message is addressed to our souls, and as such is not bound by nationality, or political or ideological affiliations. The only destiny of souls is salvation or eternal damnation.

I respect the reader's interpretation, impression and stand concerning this testimony. I do not intend to convince or to convert anyone. I am certain that only God's grace can lead us to Him. If the Lord wants to touch someone with my testimony, this will be done by His grace and mercy alone and not through the writing of my story or the experience of my kidnapping.

Before my spiritual conversion, I was convinced that I had the answers to all mystical matters and that nobody could make me change my point of view and life style. This fact made me even more interested in writing this testimony because, since my encounter, I have lived in obedience to God, facing a surprising reality that has motivated me to

Marino Restrepo

share my experience with the largest number of people possible. I realized I did not have all the answers; I also discovered that the mystical experience in my life before my conversion did not come from God but rather from darkness.

<u>Colombia, September 12, 2000</u>

I was invited to share my testimony at an upcoming Catholic spiritual retreat. From the moment I entered the place, I felt that the Lord had something very special in mind for me. After I shared my testimony, I was invited to join a silent retreat that would begin on September 12. Personally, I knew it afforded me an opportunity to have a much-needed rest for I had been giving my testimony nearly every day for about four months in different places around the country. Sometimes I had to repeat it twice or three times daily. I did not know much about spiritual retreats. I had always wanted to be in a setting like that and to participate in such an activity. It was like a secret dream come true.

At the first lecture I attended, the priest discussed the schism in the Catholic Church and explained how evidence of it could already be seen among priests and nuns of different Church branches. He spoke of the Church's need to go through a passion, crucifixion and death process in order to reach resurrection and Pentecost, since the Church is Christ's mystical body on earth. The lecturer said,

18

"The Church will suffer great tribulations and persecutions before it is purified". In other words, everything that goes to Christ belongs to Christ and turns into Christ; therefore, it goes through a Christianizing process similar to that experienced by Christ himself.

As the priest gave his lecture, I had a very deep experience. It was as if everything he was saying was already inside me, complementing and adding to the information the Lord had previously infused in me.

I realized this was a wonderful opportunity because I keenly felt that God had anointed this priest, and that the Spirit of the Lord talked through him. This encounter made me happy. Moreover, it reminded me of the period after my conversion when I returned to church and felt sorry for the incredible spiritual poverty of some of our priests and clergymen. Though many of them were highly-trained and well-educated in philosophy and theology, held high degrees and received the benefit of extensive teachings in Rome, the Holy Land and in the best universities around the world, sadly, many were, nonetheless, ignorant of the supernatural life. Seemingly, the more educated they were, the more estranged from God. I will never understand it, but I think it could be the interference of the enemy in our faith. The lecture continued, mirroring my past conversion thoughts as the priest began to discuss today's laity. My happiness knew no bounds during those moments for the priest's discussion paralleled what the Lord had earlier instilled in me. The priest also mentioned that it was the laity who would wake up the clergy and the religious communities, making them turn to the Holy Spirit and reconcile with each other.

While I listened to this man of God, something deep inside of me grew stronger: the certainty that our Lord had called me, in my adulthood, to go around the world to testify that He is alive, that our salvation was not the invention of a group of rebel Jews two thousand years ago, and that the persecution of the early Christians was really an act of martyrdom and not the action of a group of fanatics. I was attracted by the idea of bearing witness to all this and lived this first day of the retreat with an indescribable joy. The silence of all the participants contributed greatly to this wonderful experience.

I woke up the next day full of enthusiasm and went into the lecture room with my notebook and Bible. I opened up the notebook and reviewed my notes from the previous day. The priest had talked about the devil trying to sabotage God's plan to save man, and how the Holy Trinity comes to man as a perfect three-dimensional concept — an extensive and very important topic for our concept of faith. At that precise moment I felt clearly our Lord's presence telling me that those notes would be on the pages of the first book He would inspire me to write.

Following that inner revelation, the whole retreat experience took on new meaning; the more I immersed myself in it, the deeper the new dimension that presented itself — full of exciting new choices to enrich my spirit. Consequently, at this time I felt myself to be mentally absent from the opening day activities. Fortunately though, this transpired as two members of the group led the worship. There was much anointing and a cheerful spirit filled the air. The chill in the room — due to the lack of heating — gave more tenacity and character to the silence of the congregation. Cold weather in tropical highlands can be felt to the bones. I have always thought that cold weather favors concentration in intellectual activities that demand careful work and discipline.

God's perfect timing often catches us by surprise. At moments when we least expect it, He touches us, making us part of His divine pedagogy. Some people were eager to know if I had thought of writing a book about my experience with the Lord. To be honest, I had not even thought about it until the Lord inspired me. This shows that we cannot anticipate God's plans once we leave everything up to Him. Without thinking, I was already writing that book. The most difficult part was to start writing and to find a language clear enough to express everything the Lord had infused in me. It was especially difficult for me since I had not studied theology and I did not even know the catechism of the Church well. Nonetheless, difficulties no longer existed for me. I suddenly felt perfectly secure knowing that the Spirit of the Lord would guide me throughout this journey. It was clear to me that each day of this retreat would influence the first pages.

My testimony was announced for Friday of that week. This caused my relationship with the group to grow even closer. It would allow me to provide you, the reader, with a better idea of my life experience. As one more witness of conversion among the countless examples we have heard of since the dawn of Christianity over 2,000 years ago, it was my hope then, as it continues to be now, that my own life could serve to help others in their conversion.

God has a particular way of revealing Himself, every moment of each day, to all his creatures. Even though my testimony may be similar to that of others, all authentic witness lead us to one single destiny: our salvation through Our Lord Jesus Christ. It is impossible to put across a spiritual experience using mere words, or to project an immaterial and divine dimension onto a human plane. It would be like trying to feel the softness of a baby's skin wearing a thick glove. Only the grace of the Holy Spirit will allow the reader to understand the mysteries revealed to me in spite of my limited vocabulary and theological knowledge. With the blessing of our Lord and the inspiration of the Holy Spirit — spiritual guide of this journey — I invite the reader to participate in this encounter with the Lord with a joyful and humble heart and an open mind.

My life in this world, separated from God until I was 47 years old

I was born in Anserma, a coffee-growing town full of tropical charms in the Andes Mountains of Colombia. I enjoyed a healthy life there, both physically and spiritually, until I was 14 years old. My family was large, with a Catholic tradition dating back several generations. During my childhood and early teenage years I was involved in different activities in the countryside and in my hometown, and enjoyed a happy life. The sixth of ten children, I was the first boy who managed to survive. My first two brothers died very young. Three brothers and four sisters are still alive. My grandfathers, both on my mother's and my father's side, were two patriarchs who owned large coffee plantations; they were respected and admired by many, and had the political and social power that provided us with support, opportunities and protection.

My life in the church was rich and constant. Since I played the first trumpet in the school band, I got to participate in all Holy Week religious processions and this was the most exiting experience during that time. My town was located on a mountaintop, with two main streets running through it. At that time, streets were made of stone; they looked like abysses with lines of houses on both sides that reached down to the mountain base. Walking in the procession, carrying the images of saints was a real odyssey. The images had to be carried by several men since they were very big and heavy; most of them had been brought from Spain during the Colonial period. When the procession passed through one of those stone streets or abysses, there was a concern that people and statues might fall down; fortunately, nothing happened, at least during the time I participated. Town prostitutes would close down their brothels for the whole week and participate in the processions. They covered the distance on their knees, weeping and crying over their sins. They would resume their regular business on Easter Monday, as if they had paid their debt and could ask for a new loan. The rest of the inhabitants did practically the same, since their spiritual lives did not change much after Holy Week, an exception being those who were already loyal to God. You see, I grew up in the Catholic religion that by then had started to show signs of decay and which in time led many of us to the spiritual abyss our Church is in today.

In the middle of these religious contradictions, my spiritual life developed with a good dose of superstition inherited from both the Spaniards and natives. I do not think my case was any different from the rest of our Latin Christian culture. Nevertheless, I grew up in an atmosphere of good relationships with relatives and a large number of friends of my age; we were very close since we were born in a small town where everybody knew each other. All this contributed to strength in my character that would became a valuable tool in my life.

Before I was 15, I moved to Bogotá, Colombia's capital, where I lived for 5 years. I married at the age of 20, went to Hamburg, Germany, and lived there for 6 years. Then I settled in the United States where I have been since.

The years after leaving my hometown were characterized by an early rupture from my family, church and values. One or two years before leaving my town, the rumblings of a youth revolution began to reverberate from the United States and England. Elvis Presley and the Beatles started to be heard everywhere, even in distant places like Anserma.

Mass media was very limited at that time. In Colombia there was only one TV channel administered by the State and political powers. However, mass hysteria over these new idols reached all young people. Thus, my very first goal became to learn English, which I soon accomplished after moving from my uncle's house to the house of an American community called YMCA (Young Men's Christian Association) in Bogotá. I found out a couple of years later that they were Protestant. It was there where I figured out what these mysterious and powerful idols were singing and where I had the chance to meet many American students there on an exchange program.

In less than two years, everything had changed. Visiting students were no longer the clean and healthy youngsters who loved Christ and the Church, but longhaired boys and girls, dressed carelessly with bright colors, and exhibiting a strange attitude never seen before. Behind all this was the spirit of the 1960's that offered total "liberation" from the so-called "establishment". I did not understand the real meaning of all this but this weird, unconventional world that I witnessed was very attractive to my provincial spirit. Slowly, and mainly because of my first love affair with an American girl, I began to discover the secret surrounding this new attitude, this rejection of the "establishment". My girlfriend invited me to try marijuana. Under its strange sensation and effect, she began to tell me how youth would be the salvation of the world that had been corrupted by the adults. She also told me that the Vietnam War had to end and that love and peace was the only way to accomplish this.

As she conveyed all this, I could see in her beautiful blue eyes a never dreamed of promised paradise. Everything seemed so beautiful under the effect of that drug. Her beauty, combined with her 1960's vision of changing the world, were an alluring invitation to join this "legion of angels" whose mission was to save the world. Walking the streets of Bogotá, holding hands with this "heavenly missionary", I felt like I was on a cloud of happiness. I did not realize that not a soul around us could guess what we had in our hearts and even less understand the hallucination so much marijuana was causing in our brains. We would walk the streets with a group of six or seven boys and girls. I was the only Colombian in the group. They would pay for all my expenses as I could not afford their life style. Marijuana made us very hungry, necessitating many meals. We rented cars and went camping to different sites in Colombia, especially to "magical" places like pre-Columbian archaeological parks.

Although this first group of "missionary angels" was in Colombia for all of three months, it seemed but a day because of the permanent hallucinatory effects the marijuana had on us and all the 'trips' we made while high.

Free love was also talked about in those days. I had never had sexual relations with any girl before. My American girlfriend not only taught me everything about sex but also introduced me to an activity that never stopped until I found the Lord at the age of 47. The day they were about to leave, I felt as if something terrible was about to happen. What would I do without them? And so I told them, "I'll go with you". This made them all happy, particularly Donna, my girlfriend. I had my passport issued very quickly and then went to the American Embassy to get my visa. I had never been to a Consulate before and had no idea of what the process would be like. Besides, I had nothing to worry about since I was with the "saviors of the world". I was completely surprised when I discovered that "my saviors" were considered the worst criminals by their own people. A formally-dressed woman who looked like the ladies I had met at the YMCA took me to a separate room and asked mc whether any of the young men had offered me drugs like marijuana, LSD and many others I had never heard of before. I looked at her and realized how serious the situation was. "No, I have never heard of that," I retorted. She replied, "Those you are with are losers and you should not go with them anywhere; I would suggest that you go back home and carry on with your life as if you had never met them". When I left the room and looked at them, it became apparent that we had fallen off our cloud onto a hard surface called reality. I walked out holding Donna's hand, and neither she nor I spoke for quite a while. Two days later, I was completely alone after seeing them off at the airport. They gifted me the monies for my plane ticket to Miami, Donna's stereo and Beatles' music and enough marijuana to enable me to lock myself in a room for a couple of days.

My loneliness did not last long. Two days later, some knocks at the door woke me up. A new "missionary of love" named Cindy appeared in my life, and her blue eyes were even more beautiful than Donna's. Cindy had met Donna and my other friends at the airport in Miami. Cindy was on her way to Peru to visit a friend she had met in California but changed her ticket and decided to spend some time with me in Bogotá after talking to Donna and the rest of my friends. Donna had asked Cindy to be considerately loving towards me since I was very lonely. I immediately established a relationship with her as close as the one I had enjoyed with Donna; it had been Donna's idea and everything seemed to be perfect. All this was like living in a different world. How could I possibly explain the situation to the people who knew me? It was impossible.

Like Donna, Cindy also introduced me to drugs but this time to something even more extraordinary. She first asked me, "Have you ever had a trip?" A little surprised, I looked at her and said, "Only here in Colombia". She roared with laughter for quite a long time but I could not understand why. After a while she took out a big book about the ruins of the Incas. From the inside of it, she took two full pages full of round, colored circles, one page being orange dots and the other purple. She said, "Each little dot that you see here contains 400 micrograms of LSD; if you take it, you will have the most incredible mind trip, without having to go anywhere. I took about 10 trips with my friends in California, and on the last one it came to me that I had to come to South America because the magic is here in the energy of the Amazon and the secrets of the Incas." She continued to give me an esoteric lesson on South America. Then she said, "In two days, I will turn 17 and I want to celebrate my birthday with a special trip by the sea using the round, purple circle trip." I replied, "The sea is very far away from here and the ticket is very expensive". She said, "Don't worry. I'll treat you".

I lived in a never-ending fantasy that I liked more and more each day. The very next day, we were on our way to a city in Colombia's Caribbean region called Santa Marta. It was there that I experienced with Cindy the LSD trips she had talked about; they took me to a completely new dimension that I would simply describe as an opening to the doors of perception. Suffice to say, I did not manage too well (nor do I think anyone can). Most of my friends from that time went through those doors and did not come back.

Without realizing it, just over three months had passed since my initiation into the drug scene of these psychedelic messengers. The physical changes in my appearance could be readily seen. I had forgotten to shave my not-fully-developed beard and I had not had my hair cut. I wore Cindy's clothes and some of Donna's shirts and jeans. No wonder waiters thought I was a foreigner. Cindy rented a small apartment in the north of Bogotá; for me, the rent seemed astronomical but Cindy did not seem to care. Her father was a famous cardiologist in San Francisco who was providing for everything.

Cindy's apartment became the central meeting place where activities never stopped. She left me in charge of that treasure that kept everyone revolving around us: the two famous pages bearing orange and purple dots. In a few weeks, more and more Americans started to show up; they were running away from the army or came because they had heard the rumor that the best marijuana grew in Colombia. The strange thing was that we never found it. Donna and her friends had brought the first marijuana I tried from the States. Little by little, the first manuals on how to cultivate the drug, printed in San Francisco by a company called High Times, began to arrive. Soon after, the first shrubs of Colombian marijuana began to grow.

The course of my life with Cindy changed. Too many people would come to our apartment to take a "trip" for several days, and as a result, we ended up having intense love affairs with other "psychedelic angels". We became like brother and sister; this adventure in her apartment lasted two years, after which we moved to a small farm in the countryside outside of Bogotá. Then things took on a mystical dimension due to the discovery of hallucinogenic mushrooms in a place called La Miel. Located near a crystal-clear river that bore the same name, La Miel was a renowned paradise for fishermen. We turned the place into a center of psychedelic activities. It was there a few years later that a great tragedy occurred. I went there for the first time with my friends from Bogotá. Some of us stayed in that region for three months. We would eat mushrooms and talk to the trees, all the while carrying a copy of the Bible with us. When we returned to Bogotá, we found out that many of our friends were admitted to rehabilitation centers. These and many others never recovered their sanity. Psychiatrists completely ignored the effects of hallucinatory drugs and made many mistakes diagnosing some of our friends, who, in turn, were practically destroyed by erroneous treatments. Those of us who withdrew from treatment for a while did not have much trouble regaining reality after a certain time.

In two years, my hair had grown much past my shoulders and my beard was at chest-length. It was 1970 and rock-and-roll fever invaded Colombia. Hundreds of young people had run away from their homes to join different communities around the city where they lived together. In Bogotá, the "Calle Sesenta" (meaning 60th Street) became a famous psychedelic center run by eager young dealers and traders who dressed like hippies, as all of us at the time were called. Drugs like marijuana and LSD were already in the hands of dealers who were only interested in money, and who did not share the spirit of love and peace that had initially motivated the movement.

That same year, Cindy left Colombia and went back to San Francisco. She was addicted to heroin and died of an overdose. Her death broke my heart and I began to concern myself with what was going on around me. Many of our rock-and-roll heroes had died the same way, but nobody seemed to care. This new movement became increasingly intense and continued to spread all around the world.

The next and most dangerous stage began when another group of Americans introduced the tarot card, some old esoteric treatises, Voodoo and Candombe, and all sorts of practices originating from eastern paganism, including Hinduism,

Buddhism, Shintoism, Taoism and hundreds of yoga schools offering the seven levels.

All leaders of eastern paganism (or gurus, as they were known) had their heyday and dedicated themselves to conquering souls in western countries like Colombia. Occult metaphysics and all kinds of magic and superstition were the gods of the New Age who captured the peace and love spirit of the 1960's. Many of my friends in Colombia were trapped by eastern paganism to the point of becoming apostles of these sects; they created large local centers and their lives mirrored the eastern culture, especially their clothing and food choices. I was completely seduced by the supernatural fantasy of those magical, philosophical ideas. Although I studied them all with great interest, I was never a disciple or follower of any of them because my interests were more in the arts and music lines.

In the late 1960's, I met a girl with whom I shared my life for about a year; we seemed to be meant for each other. We stayed together for all that time, without having other relationships, something not normal for the lifestyle upon which I had embarked. In the course of only four years, I had had love affairs with innumerable Donnas and Cindys from all over the United States, and with a similar number of Lolas and Marias from my own country.

My last relationship came to a climax when I was 20 and my girlfriend got pregnant. Most of her family was involved in politics, worked for the government, and had a lifestyle that our own generation really hated. To them, we were the trash of the world. The news of my girlfriend's pregnancy was not well received in her family and she was advised to have an abortion. Although we were contaminated with all the magic, occultism, eastern paganism and other spiritually poisonous currents, it was impossible for us to commit such a crime. Moreover, her relatives made it very clear that they were morally superior to us. Some weeks later and after facing many difficulties, we married in a Catholic church in Bogotá. A few days later, they suggested we to go to Germany where they would help us find work. The truth is that they wanted us to be far away from them, so that we would not damage their reputation.

When we arrived in Germany in the middle of a severe winter, the first thing we had to change was our diet. Being vegetarians, we were under-nourished and that could affect the baby. Moreover, we had no idea how to follow a vegetarian diet without risking malnutrition. The same spirit flying in the skies and hearts of young Americans had influenced most young people in Germany. Without much difficulty, we joined different groups and kept the same habits for a while. After learning German, I entered the School of Liberal Arts at the University of Hamburg.

After the arrival of our first baby, our life as a couple changed due to our difficulty in coping with "the establishment" against which we had rebelled. That "establishment" hated us because of the way we dressed, thought, acted and lived. We coped by finding a neutral territory where we could enjoy the benefits offered by "the establishment" without losing our revolutionary identity of "love and peace". In order to do so, we had to change our clothes and appearance; my hair went back to almost normal; I had my beard cut, but kept a big mustache that annoyed people of "the other dimension" (as we called them). However, I managed to get a job with which to cover our basic expenses. An act of charity on the part of my wife's family led her in securing a trivial diplomatic job for the Columbian Government. We spent six years in Germany. Less than two years after our first baby was born we had our second child.

Meanwhile, my life continued to be closely related to the psychedelic world at the university through my artistic work and the music I listened to, studied and composed. I took advantage of every single opportunity that presented itself. I often traveled to Berlin and visited the traditional Kuhdam Boulevard, a set of blocks with hundreds of coffee shops, bars and rooms with small live stages side-by-side on many blocks of the boulevard. I took my guitar with me and, under the effects of drugs, played all the songs I knew to my new friends from

Europe and the United States. This way, I kept the spirit I had brought from Colombia alive, and became more esoteric, metaphysical, astrological, superstitious, spiritualistic and alchemistic. A large eastern pagan movement led all this spiritual activity. Our heroes — the Beatles and many others — were the most fervent followers of these mystical currents and had a great influence on us. It was almost impossible to meet a group of young people anywhere without hearing a magical or mystical comment of some sort. Our whole lives were guided by occultism. The only thing my wife and I shared, as a couple, was the rock-and-roll concerts. They became our focal point and we would attend them after feeding our babies. Tickets were very expensive and buying them meant not having adequate funds for everything else, but we did not care. The concerts became our church.

Little by little, the life and union between my wife and myself began to change. We no longer thought the same way. She began to feel nostalgic of her roots and I got increasingly involved in my artistic-psychedelic world. At the end of 1976, we decided to go back to Colombia. Most of our former "love and peace" friends no longer had mystical experiences. On the contrary, their lives were now focused on partying with alcohol and cocaine. To make things worse, American drug-trafficking mafias had built a paradise in Colombia from where they produced and dispatched drugs to the rest of the world. Many liquor and cigarette smugglers — unscrupulous people who were used to breaking the law and enforcing their will by killing — joined the drug business. Strong and powerful organizations appeared, and all the upper-middle class friends with whom I had shared my psychedelic life in Colombia began to finalize negotiations with American drug dealers using their knowledge of the English language and culture. A few months after arriving in Colombia, my marriage came to an end and my life started to go downhill due to my use of alcohol, cocaine, the bad deals I had made and my lustful nature, sparked by the use of all these drugs.

I went to the United States where I began a troubled and confused life — separated from my love of the arts and music. I spent some time in Florida and New York; my life became immersed in a world of bars, cocaine and women who were as decadent as I — a world full of anxiety due to the separation from my children and wife. Nothing seemed to fill that emptiness. My spiritual life that I viewed as the last step on a magical ladder — full of gifts and power — was no more than a devil's sham, but I was completely unaware of that at that time. Later on, my artistic connections and acquaintances in New York led me to start a new life in California. I got involved in an activity that would take 20 years of my life and that kept me moving between the cinema, television and music, in a world of drugs and lust. Hollywood seemed to be the great Mecca for this type of life. The same spirit that had baptized me to the world of Donna in Colombia, through that first marijuana cigarette in 1967, was still orienting my life in California. It was no coincidence that coming from the same dark force, it would beckon me, giving one last shake before leaving me in perpetual spiritual darkness.

My artistic life began again in California and helped me somehow to fill the emptiness and anxiety that had caused me to waste away during the previous four years. At the same time, my magical and esoteric activity increased considerably. California could well be the world center of the New Age movement and its spiritual darkness. Esoteric prophets, new metaphysical or spiritualistic sects, the most important centers of satanic masonry, along with the most active satanic churches of America were — and still are — thriving in California. Many evil characters had infiltrated Hollywood as famous writers working for the most prestigious film studios, or as producers of the greatest movies ranging from Disney's productions for children to Warner Brothers' horror movies. This spirit began to grow in the 1960's when the "love and peace" generation was born, and has increased ever since in San Francisco Bay. The most obscure movements are promoted from Hollywood; they are shown as entertainment, as fantasy, as an expression of the seventh art, whose only purpose is to supposedly enrich our daily lives. Much could be said about this topic, but I would have to ask the Lord to give me the opportunity to write another book on this vast and obscure subject.

In 1986, a partner from Colorado (with whom I composed several songs over the span of two years) and I managed to sign a contract with Sony Music in New York (CBS Records at that time). Our contract was for five records and the operating budget was favorable. This opened a new chapter in my artistic life; the long worldwide tours we undertook illustrate the advantages that few multinational companies can afford to offer. A few months after signing the contract, my wife arrived from Colombia on a surprise visit to tell me that she had been diagnosed with cancer. The news made me very sad; in spite of our separation of several years, we were still somewhat like husband and wife, enjoying a good friendship and having a lot of respect for each other. In other words, we were best friends because we knew each other's life perfectly and there were no secrets between us.

A few months later, we decided it would be better for our children to live with me since she was already very ill and could not take care of them properly. By then, they were young teenagers. This meant a big change in my lifestyle. Initially the children went to a boarding school for a year. Then they came to live with me permanently. My frequent music tours made the first years very difficult. In a way, this new responsibility of taking care of my children made me abandon many destructive activities in which I had previously engaged that were leading me towards an abyss. In 1992, my wife, after much suffering, died in Colombia. The cycle of emotions and experiences of my former life that began in the 1960's had come to a close.

Notwithstanding, I was still involved in occult practices. In 1993, my youngest brother died in a sea accident on the island of Antigua under unknown circumstances. Six months later, my father also passed away from a brain hemorrhage. In 1996, only two years after these deaths, another brother shot himself to death during an argument with his wife after having consumed some alcohol at a party. Two months later, my mother died in my arms, totally emaciated by all these family tragedies. After being notified of my brother's death at the end of 1996, I flew to Colombia for the funeral. It was held in Pereira, a small city located in the coffee-growing region of Colombia, an hour's drive from our hometown. My mother had been living there for the past 35 years.

It was not easy going back to Colombia after a fourteen-year absence. The country had changed a lot in every aspect; even the currency changed in appearance. Some things had changed for the better, like the number of job opportunities, but other things were worse than before, as evidenced by the violence, intolerance and moral decay in all levels of society.

Seeing my sisters again after several years was rather difficult because of the situation we were going through. My mother who was still living at the time was so full of grief that it was almost impossible to look into her eyes. My brother's funeral took place about four hours after I arrived. I was very surprised to see so many relatives in the church. I had not been exposed to such a gathering, or even to a funeral, since I was a child. I had forgotten that my family was so large. The days that followed were sad and full of grief for my sisters and me. Our mother was now terminally ill and there was nothing we could do for her but wait, since doctors had given up all hope of her recovering. I was so distant from God that the word miracle was neither part of my vocabulary, nor that of my sisters. People, including my own family, seemed to go very often to church. However, their spiritual qualities were not really evident. Religion did not seem to have changed in all those years. It seemed quite the same to me. Two months later, after enduring long nights of anguish, my mother died. I could still feel the smell of incense from the last funeral, and there we were again, attending another one even more painful and difficult than the last. After these two funerals, my sisters and I talked about who would be the next since we were heading toward death in a very close sequence. In less than four years, five members of my family had died.

In the year that followed, I adopted the food habits and easy-going, bohemian lifestyle that was common in Colombia. While experiencing this idealism that was no more than ancestral nostalgia, I flew between Los Angeles and Colombia three more times before my eventual kidnapping. My last trip before being kidnapped was in November of 1997. I wanted to spend Christmas with my sisters to share the sadness with them caused by the absence of so many relatives.

To be honest, now that I look back, I see that the biggest attraction for me in Colombia was the intensive party-life in small towns like mine. While driving along the busy highways of Los Angeles, the only thought that came to my mind was being in the arms of one of those beautiful and "easy-going" girls that abound in Colombia. Alcohol, drugs and women were still controlling my life. My only thoughts were in that direction and I felt I could easily satisfy them in Colombia.

I arrived in Colombia that Christmas full of enthusiasm for the upcoming Christmas carnival that would last until January 14th. I had to be back in Los Angeles on that day to begin a four-week U.S.A. tour with my band. For the past three years I had been experiencing financial difficulties due to my involvement in the film merchandising business.

Hollywood produces all sorts of merchandise to promote films, and this industry has become gigantic worldwide. Thanks to the contacts I had made for so many years, I had managed to obtain exclusive deals. That Christmas I had particular commitments with many investors. Our business had serious problems with the IRS and the entire investment was in jeopardy. I was responsible for many people's money. However, everything seemed to be under control. I did not know at the time that I would soon be kidnapped and held hostage for six months in the jungles of Colombia.

On December 11th I arrived in Pereira where my mother had died and three of my four sisters were still living. I began to plan great parties for those days. In the afternoon of December 25th, I left for my hometown, all the while feeling very tired and dizzy as a result of the party we had had on Christmas Eve which lasted until 7 a.m. After driving for less than an hour, I arrived in Anserma and went to visit friends and relatives until midnight. I was so tired that I had no energy to drink or dance anymore. In this region of the country, Christmas parties go on for several days. At midnight, I left to spend the night at an uncle's farm located near the south entrance to the town, close to the urban area. When I arrived, I was surprised to find the gate closed, for my uncle would always leave it open when he knew I was coming. One of my nephews was with me and I asked him to get out of the car to open the gate. The moment he opened it, a group of men holding guns, with their heads covered, jumped out of the darkness. A few seconds later, they put my nephew in the rear seat of my car. They opened all the doors and, like hungry dogs, looked for anything they could find. They forced me out of the car, tied my hands, covered my head and took all my belongings.

At first, I thought I was being robbed, a crime very common in Colombia. Then the situation grew worse. The six men got into my car, made me sit in the back seat, and began driving down the road at high speed. Once we were out of town, they stopped the car; four of them got out and took me with them, while the other two left with the car, taking my nephew with them. Being left on the road and without knowing what was going on, I started to think that they were going to kill me and dispose of my body somewhere in the mountains. But that was not their plan. They tied a rope around my waist which two men held, one from the front and one from the back. Then they made me walk through the mountains all night long with the hood still covering my head.

We arrived at what seemed to be the main house of an abandoned farm in the countryside and they took me to what sounded like an empty room, judging by the echo. I was left there alone for the rest of the day; late at night they took me out, led me to a road and put me again in the rear part of a car in which we rode for a long time. I heard them saying that the police and the army were looking for me, and so they had to take me to another place. After a long trip at high speed on an unpaved and very bumpy road, my body was left in bad shape since I could not avoid banging and hitting myself against the car. As a result of this ordeal, my body was bleeding and bruised all over. Then we got out of the car and began to walk again for several hours; this time I could tell we were in the jungle because instead of hearing urban birds singing, I heard sounds that could only be heard deep in the jungle. Although I had been born in a small town and lived as a child in the countryside, walking tied up and blindfolded in the jungle at night made me very nervous and increased the panic caused by this terrible odyssey.

The humidity made it difficult for me to breathe through the acrylic hood that covered my head. This affected the circulation in my blood, causing my arms and back to hurt. The alcohol I had consumed for the last three days had sapped all my energy; each step made me feel closer to a heart attack. Many hours later that seemed like an eternity, we finally arrived at our destination. They removed my hood to show me my new surroundings. The situation seemed to get more and more complicated. The place they showed me was not exactly the Ritz Carlton Hotel. It was a house that had been abandoned a long time ago and was now overgrown with trees with branches coming out of what should have been windows and doors. It seemed more like a cave than a house. They covered my head again and steered me to the cave and threw me into it. Upon landing, I heard a lot of fluttering and realized that I was surrounded by thousands of bats. The floor on which I had fallen was rotten and covered with bat excrement. I did not know what was worse: the smell of the cave, the mixture of rotting substances or the constant rain of excrement that increased every time I moved. The threat of being attacked by all those winged creatures reminded me of Alfred Hitchcock's film, "The Birds."

At the same time, thousands of bugs came out of the excrement and crawled into my clothes, biting me from head to toe. Each bite produced a different itch. Some of them felt like electric shocks; others produced big skin inflammations all over my body, while still others caused intense itching. They all felt like separate attacks, injecting their own brand of poison. Soon, my whole body was completely covered with a variety of bites and inflammations. I could not scratch myself since my hands were still tied up. The lack of circulation in my arms made my body numb. I did not move because I was afraid to disturb the bats again. My situation could not have been worse. My first days transpired in this way: isolated, in much pain, in utter darkness, even unable to untie my hands; I did not want to receive the food I was offered once a day. All I desperately wanted was to finish this ordeal and die. On the third day, a small hope of being able to escape arose in me. I started to call for my captors, thinking that they might remove me from this cave and once outside I might have a chance to escape. I called for them. I had no energy and my voice was failing me. The idea of causing panic among the 'dwellers' of the cave with the least movement prevented me from further efforts.

After a while, one of the captors came. I don't know whether it was to give me something to eat or if he had heard my voice. He pulled me out by my feet — something they had not done before — took the hood off and asked me if I wanted something to eat. I could not see anything for a while. I was afraid to open my eyes since I had been completely blinded by the darkness of the cave for three days. Afterwards, I realized it was sunset. The soft sunlight allowed me to look inside the cave.

I became even more afraid when I saw the extended array of spider webs that had probably been there for several years. I had never seen anything of this magnitude before. They looked like the curtains of a big, macabre stage scene. Their surface was covered with a greenish slime. Slowly I began to observe the biggest and most hairy spiders I had ever seen. They seemed to know that I was looking at them. I realized I had made a big hole in one of those large spider webs where I had been laying for the last three days.

The captor who took me out of the cave explained that they had no food because the group that was supposed to pick me up hadn't arrived yet. He did not say whom they were waiting for or what they were planning to do with me. I did not dare ask any questions. I had lost all hope of surviving and — just to get it over with — felt like running away so they would capture and kill me quickly. However, I did not have the strength to do so.

After a while, another criminal arrived with a bunch of green plantains and a can he probably had found nearby, with dirty water for me to drink. I suppose that under different circumstances anyone who had neither eaten nor drunk for several days would have considered the offer a real feast. However, I felt very weak and was not interested. When they noticed that I did not accept their food, they again put the hood on and bound my hands, this time at the front, which helped my blood circulation.

The two men reminded me of a pair of hungry wolves that had finally hunted their prey down, and after searching around found a cave where to hide it, in order to share it later with the rest of the pack. Then they threw me back into the cave. Twelve days passed and no one appeared. Sometimes I could hear them arguing, and saying that they would wait one more day for them to appear or they would have to kill me. Thank God they did not. I had no idea what this was all about. Every other day, they would come and give me something to eat, which I began to accept. Living in that cave turned me into another bat. I had already learned the communication system between adults and their young bats; those high-frequency sounds gave me severe headaches since I was in the middle of that signal traffic. The excrement that fell during the day, after the early morning feeding time, had a horrible smell and increased the activity of all those bugs on the floor whose feeding zone included me. Sometimes I could feel huge armies of bugs coming into the cave to get some food for their own group. I could almost understand the negotiations that took place in order to decide the type and size of the prey they would take out, which included my skin and blood.

One night, after spending 15 days in this hellish cave, I heard a large group of people arriving at night. They grabbed me, untied my hands and removed my hood. I felt great relief. My blood began to circulate again causing me great pain and many cramps. However, being out of the cave, untied and free of the hood was like being in heaven even though their intentions involved killing me. Suddenly nearly 80 men wearing military clothes surrounded me. I could easily notice that they were not military soldiers; they rather looked like a group of actors in a Poncho Villa's film. Yet, this was real life. They all appeared to be under 18. The only man that seemed to be over 30 began to talk.

This man did not look at me while speaking; he kept moving around me. In a voice loud enough for all to hear, he explained that I had been kidnapped and sold to them by the men who had taken me to the cave. He identified himself as the commander of the group that belonged to one of the largest guerrilla-groups in Colombia.

This caricature-like commander showed me a list with the names of all my sisters, their correct addresses and telephone numbers. He told me I would have to pay him an incredibly large amount of money as ransom. He also stated that that was just a small amount of the fortune I supposedly had. Then he went on telling me that my initial kidnappers wanted me dead after the ransom was paid, because they were afraid of me going after them since they were from my hometown and I had recognized them. I found out later that these men belonged to a well-known family from my village that had failed in the drug-trafficking business, and that they were paying off their debts by kidnapping people. The commander threatened to kill my sisters one by one if I refused to pay the ransom they requested. I cannot express in words everything that went through my mind while being the focal point of this absurd trial on a dark night in the middle of the jungle. My emotions underwent subtle changes:

from anger to fear, pain to anguish, revenge to bravery. I could feel the look of all those malnourished jackals preying on me, without having enough flesh to feed them all. Everything that ridiculous commander said was celebrated with laughter by these jackals. After a while, he offered me a drink of aguardiente (strong Colombian liquor). He ordered his men to tie me up again and return me to the cave blindfolded. He said they would be back in one or two days to take me to another locale. The six men who had originally sold me disappeared and another group of youths stayed on guard outside the cave. Everyone else had left.

My Mystical Experience Led by the Vision and Revelation of Our Lord

One hour after I was sent back to the cave, my experience became worse than that of the previous fifteen days. Deep within me I was hoping to survive this horrible experience, but all hope disappeared after my encounter with these criminals. I was in a situation where one simple error on my part could not only cause my death but also that of my sisters. This complicated matters even more. Not only was I the one in trouble, but my family too. From that moment on, I had to be very careful. It was a fact that my death sentence was dictated to me in the most cruel and hard way. There was no doubt that I considered myself a dead man, but I didn't know when and how I was going to be executed. No words can describe the horror I experienced. Suddenly, my entire life crumbled in front of me and I could only contemplate the ashes of what was left of it. I couldn't conceive, for an instant, how absurd it was to be in a jungle in Columbia not too far from the town where I was born and which I had departed thirty-three years earlier.

My glamorous life that I had just left behind in Hollywood, my travels throughout the world, and all my goals and ambitions were suddenly reduced to a pile of ashes. Nothing could change the reality of this moment no matter how transcendental the experience could have been. Even money could not have solved this problem because after paying the ransom they were going to execute me anyway. I didn't even have one third of the money they wanted from me.

An immense loneliness enveloped my being and a great desperation covered the whole universe around and inside of me. I couldn't even express the turmoil and pain I felt. Tied up with my head covered in a hood, I was incapable of walking or making any type of movement that would give me a little air or add hope to my indescribable pain. My anguished soul was looking for support, something that would give me the comfort I so desperately needed. None of my past life experiences, especially the spiritual ones that I had previously considered to be beacons of great wisdom and perhaps even holy, came to my rescue. Not one single magical presence from my past could offer any assistance including: magic formulas, esoteric treaties, metaphysical knowledge of the occult, mantras (on other occasions these had brought me inner peace), astrological charts (only two months earlier these had presented a picture of great success), crystals that I brought from many parts of the world with the purpose of protecting my physical and spiritual integrity, and all sorts of mysterious amulets that were given to me in the midst of great rituals. Supposedly inundated with mysticism, so many of these amulets had been brought back from the four corners of the earth throughout the years. At this time though, absolutely nothing came to my rescue.

Where were all the spirits that for so many years had never failed to guide me through my spiritual exercises (spiritualism)? I had no option other than to abandon myself completely into the hands of what appeared to be the unending abyss of a final journey. The crucial culminating moment of all my past experiences had arrived. It is hard to imagine that what was beginning to happen at this moment could be called an encounter with God. The first thing I saw with clarity was a moment in my childhood that occurred on the inside patio of the home in which I was born. Remember, I had spent the past fifteen days in total darkness. All that was visible to me was my mind to which I could not close my inner eyes no matter how much I tried. Fully awake, I was very conscious of the macabre room, which was infested with bats and millions of insects and bugs.

To see my childhood so clearly depicted filled me with anguish and desperation. I was 47 years of age and couldn't explain how I could see myself so clearly after that many years. What was happening to me? Was I going insane? Little by little as my life unfolded with precise clarity, an immense pain began to envelop me. It grew stronger as each bad action over the past years was disclosed. The revelation made such an impression that I thought I was hallucinating from the poisonous bites of the insects and bugs. Something deep inside of me was conscious of what was actually taking place and it was as being aware that I had been kidnapped and was in the jungle. I was afraid to accept that reality because I didn't understand its origin. In agony, after reliving practically my whole life, my first thought was that this was nothing but a walk back into my past. However, the truth of this incredible experience could not be hidden. My heart was very much aware that my soul knew a lot.

As the first image of my childhood unfolded, I found myself on a tricycle. With a stick in my hand I was going around in circles in the interior of the house, hitting all the plants. Each subsequent image appeared with the same clarity. Suddenly though, something happened that only the Holy Spirit in the heart of the reader can explain because words are simply inadequate. I found myself lying face down on the grass immersed in the freshness of a very friendly field. I lifted my head and looked to the right and saw a mountain. On top of the mountain was a small but vibrantly lit-up city, filled with apparent life. It was not lit up because it was night as there was no sense of day or night. In that instant I heard an incredible voice that transformed my very existence the moment it began speaking to me — a voice so majestic that not even a million words could describe it. If I took all the psalms that praise the Lord there wouldn't be enough beauty to do justice to describe such a voice.

I looked to the left and saw my body as though through a curtain of smoke. I was lying in that macabre room tied up with a hood covering my head. The first thing I felt in my heart was that I had just left this world. Yet, I didn't feel dead; on the contrary, I had never felt more alive than at that very moment. Gone were my aches and pains. No longer was I filled with fear or anguish. It seemed that I had a body. I could see in the distance the only body; I knew it was mine. The voice I heard was not human. It was the voice of Our Lord. No one could speak that way. It seemed to come from everywhere and at the same time from within me. It filled everything around me.

The Lord confirmed that He was the originator of the communication when He said, "I am going to show you the precise moment you began to walk away from me." He wasn't intimidating me. I felt only an infinite love, an eternal security. I was in the hands of one from which I had nothing to fear, someone I could only love and from whom I could receive love. There was no sense of time or space

57

even though I was observing the mountains, the lit-up city and the grass. Nothing seemed to be; it was as though everything seemed to exist without being united but everything was on hold at the same time.

The Lord proceeded to give me a long and detailed lesson on the material world and my relationship with it. Every time He referred to the world concerning any given event in my life I was transported to that lit-up city. Here I would show up on stage in the midst of His examples and teachings. The Lord conveyed to me that never in the history of humanity has the world been so far away from Him. The state of idolatry has surpassed every single human cycle of the past that might be registered in the history of the sacred scriptures. Our spiritual bankruptcy is of alarming dimensions.

Industrial progress, the technological achievements and all the sociological findings reflect in equal proportions the immense spiritual bankruptcy of humanity, a current generation void of heaven's light, seduced and consumed by a transitory and illusory life which seeks to conquer self. Little by little these centers of materialism have crumbled the spiritual structure that was edified with the blood of the Lamb and with that of thousands of martyrs in the first 400 years of Christianity. Humanity is so far away from the Lord that the great majority of mankind dedicates itself exclusively to feeding the human body which is going to die, and is completely oblivious to nourishing the spirit that will live forever. People are so involved in the material world that a great majority of souls stand in the presence of God in a state of spiritual malnutrition. Like handicapped souls they are incapable of facing God's light. The journey of the soul during this life in the flesh should be oriented towards achieving spiritual health in order to·attain eternal life in the spirit.

If the life in the flesh was in conformity with the spirit, we could benefit by a spiritual growth that would give us the grace to find union with God at the moment of death (the maximum realization of the creature being fused with his Creator never to be separated again). Every instant in the life of the spirit while walking incarnate through this transitory world is a space in time that can be marked for eternal benefits if it is lived in harmony with God. At the same time, every instant that one lives in the body (flesh) without communion with the spirit is a period of time that has been separated from God in eternity as well.

The Lord explained to me how important it is for us to establish a perfect communion between flesh and spirit and to understand first and foremost something basic about the wisdom of our spiritual existence. Heaven, purgatory, hell and this material world exist at the same time in the spiritual plateau. Therefore, we have to be conscious that in this very moment and at the instant at which we were conceived in the womb of our earthly mother, we are standing in eternity. All our actions permanently endure in eternity. Only when we establish harmony with the spirit, after we have not been in harmony with it, can we (while still in the flesh) change the disharmonious relationship that we previously had into a harmonious one, restoring all the moments that we lived disconnected from the spirit. We can call these 'unloving moments.'

We can achieve this restoration only while we are still in the flesh because at the moment we die and leave the flesh, we go from the state of grace to the state of justice. In the state of justice the soul is naked, stripped from the flesh, sustained only in what it spiritually achieved while in this earthly life. All the empty spaces of love, unfulfilled during the walk of life, have to be filled in the new state. The spiritual body must be perfectly illuminated before he is able to see the beatific vision that is the Creator; otherwise he enters the state called purgatory.

The soul that no longer possesses a sinful flesh recognizes the Creator as Lord and has rebuked the devil but is not in a perfect state of purity nor in a state of perfect illumination, is in a holy state. However it must strive for the rehabilitation of the spiritual body that is impure because of the imperfect relationship between spirit and flesh during the period of grace. In order to find the divine — the perfect that exudes holiness — we have to achieve the maximum state of purity

The incredible spiritual ignorance in which humanity finds itself based on what the Lord showed me is such that our present times are worse than Babylon and Sodom and Gomorrah. Sin, rather than being an act of transgression, is a way of life. Everything has been justified so that we can live totally unattached to the Ten Commandments. The soul's state is in bankruptcy. Humans lack knowledge of the real presence of the devil in their lives. The Lord is referring to those who should know this due to having received the grace of the Holy Spirit through baptism. Those who have not been baptized in Christ, such as pagans, Jews or Muslims, are going to be called to Divine Justice according to the spiritual talents that the Lord has given them. The sad part is that the vast majority of Christians — over two billion — are not aware of the gospel and do not have the grace-filled teachings of Christ that are in the New Testament — the perfect map of salvation — present in their lives.

Satan is viewed as something metaphoric — far from daily reality. According to the Lord, what is worse is that the Church itself in great proportions has been overlooking the teachings of the knowledge of the enemy to the point where the word 'exorcism' is cause for persecution and discrimination within the Church itself. All this is because of the convenient accommodation that has been given to the gospel to please the world and the protestantization of the Catholic Church due to fear of being ridiculed by the world which looks for what is politically correct rather than what is the right devotion.

The teaching of Christ concerning the evil one is so extensive in the gospel that the Lord says it is absolutely absurd that the Church could ignore these teachings. This should occupy a very important and vital place in any catechesis. If we don't recognize that walking through this transitory and material world is a battle for the life or death of the soul, then we are wasting all the graces we received by Our Lord Jesus Christ who is the Key, the True Path and the Conqueror of Eternal Life.

The greatest trap that is laid down by the enemy is to make humanity believe that eternal life begins when the flesh dies and not during this life in the flesh. If there is something that Jesus has liberated us from, it is the immense error planted by the enemy in the oriental pagan religions who believe in reincarnation. Through the occult and pagan practices of the east, humans have been estranged from this teaching of Christ century after century. Christ taught us that we only live once in the flesh. The soul only returns to another material body at the moment of the last judgment, at which time a perfect physical body will be given.

The enemy's astuteness at always imitating what is divine is meant to confuse man. Satan takes the knowledge that he received as an angel, the understanding that we are united in a single body to a single tree since original sin, and therefore that all our ancestors are united with us not only in genetic but also in spiritual form. Satan subverted this concept into reincarnation.

The fact that we carry within us information on the history of the flesh since Adam and Eve leads Satan through regression to show us all the lives in the flesh. Many people believe that those lives are of that same spirit when in reality they are the ones of our ancestors who are united to the same human tree. The Lord showed me how we are a single tree; each one of us is a branch that grows as far back as our forefathers, Adam and Eve. Through that branch we receive millions of blessings as a consequence of the good actions of our ancestors. The oriental pagans refer to it as karma or the law of cause and effect. We also receive curses that are for a limited number of generations. This is also referred to as karma in the Far East.

The Lord showed me a river that He compared to the flesh. For example, if we submerge our hand into the Amazon River at its source in the Peruvian Andes, we are touching the same water in the

Amazon River that flows through Columbia; if we submerge our hand in the Amazon River that flows through Brazil, we are touching the same body of water that flows through Columbia and Peru. It is an extensive river through the same water. So it is with human flesh, says the Lord. An immense river of sinful human flesh flows from its source — Adam and Eve.

The Lord explained to me that He takes human flesh, unites divinity with humanity, submerges it into the river of sin, crucifies it, resurrects it and through it repairs the sin of man from the moment of birth until the last current that flows until His return.

The Lord said that an immense portion of humanity today is a product of fornication rather than love. Millions of humans are conceived in the midst of the most abominable sins. A large majority of these people are rejected in their mother's womb and millions of them aborted. Those born into a loveless world drag with them the weight not only of original sin but also the abomination of the sins of their parents.

It is true that we inherit the blessing of being baptized in Christ our Lord and we are pardoned and freed from every attachment of our ancestors and from the sin of our forefathers. It is also true that when we reach the age of reason and begin to sin we lose this grace and return to the roots of evil in which we were born, and there are also new chains put upon us through our individual personal sin. Sin cannot be inherited because we have been given the freedom to choose between good and evil. However, the Lord pointed out that we do inherit the consequences of sin.

Due to this massive absence of love in so many millions of human beings who are born in the midst of the most horrible sins, the world couldn't be darker. We are inundated by resentment, hatred, hearts that are abandoned and stepped on even before they come out of their mother's womb, a humanity that in its majority tries to resolve the pain it carries by inflicting pain on others with a self-destructing nature. As such, they create an environment of vice, death and desolation. The same sin that penetrated the flesh through sexual impurity turns into the very essence that is none other than death, not only death of the material body but also the death of the soul. It is a humanity that has surrendered to the great falling of the spirit through the flagellation inflicted by lust, vice, greed and idolatry of the flesh, while being a slave to the material world that searches in vain to fill the deepest void created by the absence of God with an endless sea of desires, anxieties, vain goals, revenge and violence itself as a way of life. A son born without love turns into a fire of violence and hatred. Nothing can fill the void that is left by the absence of God. The only thing that we can retain from this existence is the love that we gave during our lifetime. If we detach ourselves from the slavery of the human condition and elect to live within our eternal nature using every instant of our life as a treasure of reparation and capitalization in the great economy of the salvation of the soul, we will begin to deposit real money in the only existing royal bank, the bank of heaven. That money is love, the true heir and essence of eternal life that has been given to us.

The Lord showed me with sadness a humanity that has come too close to the edge of its own abyss of eternal destruction. Despite this the Lord emphasizes that we are all His children and, as such, have the right to salvation regardless of the state of sin in which our soul finds itself. The devil cannot seize an incarnate soul completely. At the moment of death that soul has the opportunity to renounce sin and recognize God, saving itself even though it will remain in an alarming state of purification. The Lord said that when a baby is born of the flesh, another baby is born with him and is called soul. Both coexist in a perfect union with God and the spirit of the Lord is the womb of that soul.

Today, a great number of human creatures from the moment they achieve financial stability, human affection, power or ways of pleasure, turn to selfishness, pretension, vanity, pride, greed or lust in such a way that the spirit of the Creator is left behind and the spirit of evil enters the soul, adopting it as a daughter to educate and later bury eternally at the end of its material life. The relationship between creature and Creator breaks down the moment the creature believes to have control of his own life. At that moment intimacy begins with the destructor who provides ever more fervently the confidence that the existence of the deceived creature depends on itself and nothing else. The highest state of willfulness possesses the being, turning it into an idol of its own selfishness, the temple of its self-sufficiency.

It is definitely important to understand that we have to identify in whose territory we are standing, whether we are in God's territory or the devil's. There is no such thing as half a saint or half a demon. We either belong to God or to the devil. If we are in God's territory, it is the Holy Spirit that encases the soul. We live within the bosom of God in spite of living incarnate in a material body because of original sin. The soul can still remain permanently united with God from this material life onwards if it so chooses; on the other hand, the soul not in union with God turns into Satan's latrine where the devil deposits his excrement (sin) day by day.

The Lord showed me my childhood and the first step I took in my walk away from Him. He took my

47-year old heart and connected it with my 3-year old heart, not to tell me that the first step I took away from Him was a conscious one but to show me how a perverse life could lead a thinking man so far away from God. Beginning with my own family, which supposedly knew the values of a Christian life, the Lord showed me how contaminated humanity is today. He took me back to my childhood home where I was surrounded by my parents, brothers and grandfather. Grandpa was giving me a beautiful toy, a fire truck that was lavishly gift-wrapped in a way that would impress any small child. Having to wait until the long ceremony was over before receiving my gift caused me great anguish, as I wanted that toy so badly. After what seemed like eternity, it was finally given to me.

To a 3-year old child, knowing where a toy came from or what it is made of is unimportant. The only intention in such an innocent heart is to play with the toy. To an adult, however, the toy is an object of vanity. The giver of the gift is unconsciously filled with pride, as are those adults who witness the giving process.

Much importance is given to that gift. By the time the child finally receives it, the gift has gone from being a toy to being his first possession. It is an object that will exact a price such as having to share it with others, something that you cannot take away from the child without causing him to cry, or need to bargain and trade it for another attractive object. It is difficult to understand the gravity of interchange between an adult and a child. The Lord showed me that this was the first step in my growth to attachment and the slavery of material things. Obviously this is not the case with every gift and toy. If we lived in harmony with our Lord we would have the necessary discernment and wisdom to raise our children without turning them into slaves of materialism.

As the Lord took me through my childhood, He showed me step by step how I was slowly becoming attached to the external world, abandoning my relationship with the Holy Spirit that until then had permeated my entire existence. I was beginning to lose joy, security and love and was gradually turning into a person who was constantly depending on human affection with an appetite geared towards the senses and instincts. He showed me how profoundly our attachments develop towards our parents, friends and everyone who enters our life, our places of residence and our environment.

The Lord showed me how spiritually handicapped I was at 16 years of age due to the extensive roots I had developed with the world. As a result my existence was absolutely terse and plain, filled with anxieties and the desires of nature. In essence, it was nothing more that the absence of God in me.

With infinite sadness I witnessed the separation from the grace that was given to me at birth. Most important were the moments where growth was wasted as I began to damage the senses of the spirit by trying to satiate the senses of the flesh with no future to be expected other than death.

It is true that due to original sin we are born blind, deaf and mute to the spirit until we are stripped of the flesh. However, if we grow in harmony with the spirit, our eyes will be filled with faith and like a compass will guide our path through this desert — our exile. In the midst of this sad lesson, the Lord showed me how the material world can be an instrument of salvation or damnation depending on how we use it. He has given this material world to us in order that we minister to His honor and glory, and serve humanity.

As we grow up the material world begins to dominate us and we find ourselves walking further and further away from the territory of God, submerging ourselves more and more into the territory of Satan — prince of this world. We lose our independence as well as our spiritual, mental and physical health. Our weaknesses control us. Sexuality becomes the veil that replaces devotion.

The more I reviewed my life through the eyes of the Lord, the more pain I felt. My greatest agony was discovering in this examination that the key to heaven is the cross of Calvary of our Lord Jesus Christ.

The world that I created was totally oriented towards avoiding pain and attaining comfort and pleasure at any price — a reality that every day made it more and more impossible to conceive that suffering, pain and tribulation are the true path of absolute union with God and a way of purification. Moreover, when our existence focuses only on our mortal life we can see the first step to human tragedy. Our goal will be to attain happiness in this world. Thus, it is impossible to attain simply because there cannot be full realization in what is not permanent. It is like trying to build a house on the waves of the ocean.

When I reviewed my life in Germany at age 23, a new wave of sadness overcame me. Despite living an apparently detached life from the material world because of the new culture of peace and love and my rejection of what was known as "the establishment," in reality I was no different from any of the people I used to protest against. I was equally filled with unruly appetites of the flesh, wanting things of the world and completely seduced by the proposals of the devil. Man sometimes fills himself with moral scruples, false dogmas of faith and apparent spiritual disciplines to cover up the mold that he carries and to feel free of sin and contamination. This is the same as a person who doesn't shower but uses fine perfumes and wears the most sophisticated clothes. It doesn't matter how much you try and cover the dirt, it will not leave you until you bathe and clean up.

The mystery of the cross is the greatest spiritual treasure that exists. While the Lord was reviewing my life, at least a thousand times I noticed the way my eyes were riveted on the cross in so many places I had passed by during the years that I was away from God. Regardless of the circumstance, I could appreciate how every time I stared at the crucifix, I felt a deep burning call inside of me. Unfortunately, since I was so deaf to the grace of the Holy Spirit, none of this filtered through; none of these encounters with the cross touched me. Based on what the Lord infused in me about this mystery, today I see a great majority of Christians carrying their cross upside down. The true sense of faith is not to bring our sorrows or tribulations to the crucified Lord in order for our problems to be solved immediately. Nor is it to kneel before the cross and complain about our weaknesses. To act so is to carry our cross upside down.

First, and foremost, we have to understand something very important. Heaven does not send us anything bad or evil. God won't take our car or our job away from us. He won't send us a divorce or break up an effective relationship. He will not send sickness upon us. The fountain of all tribulation is sin. Sin is the evil one who at the same time charges a fine in the flesh and in the material life to those who step on his territory and eat his infernal bread and wine. The enemy that tempted us, led us into sin and later turned tribulation into sickness and calamity, is the administrator of our transgressions.

Many of the sins that affect our lives from our early years are consequences of the acts of our ancestors. We only receive these afflictions because of the fact that we have lost the grace acquired through baptism; nonetheless, we revert to the inherent sins and those we willfully committed. The real calling to Christians is to present ourselves at the foot of our crucified Lord. This means bringing Him everything so that He can receive, purify and repair any damage in order to finally free us. We should come before Him and say: *"Lord, at your crucified feet I come to prostrate myself to give you this pain, suffering, anguish, trial, disease, whatever the affliction may be. I want you, Lord, to receive it so that you can make it Your Will. I know that you didn't send me this particular trial but I also know that you taught us the way of Calvary. You call us to carry our own cross and to unite it with yours. Make of my pain whatever you will. Let this contribute to the salvation of my soul, my family and whatever intentions you may have when you receive this. Glory to you, Almighty Lord. If you want to heal me, save me from this trial, this disease and this pain. Glory to you, Lord."*

This is the real communion with the cross. Just as Christ united the divine with the human when He became man, so too we have to unite our humanity with the divine by becoming more like Christ. At that moment we will have defeated the devil. We can be assured that Satan will be furious for a long time. The intention of the enemy, when he castigates us with the discovery of our sin, is to distance us from God, and lead us to despair. We cannot believe for an instant that the enemy will stop looking for us once we find the true path of the cross, for his goal is not our purification but rather our destruction. Moreover, every time we sin we incur a debt; Satan is intent on making sure we pay our dues for each sin committed down to the last cent. This may sound absurd coming from someone like me who used to laugh at divine law but now I know that when we are separated from grace all our thoughts and actions are conceived in the bosom of evil and that is why we cannot see or understand the language of God. The worst sin of humanity is to have consented to sin to the extreme. The disintegration of the relationship with God leads to further transgressions. The sinner becomes his own lawmaker on this path that leads to a destiny where grace is excluded.

The Lord views the world we live in today as a universe divorced from grace drowning in its own spiritual disgrace. Did not the Lord say: "Carry your cross and follow me"? Consider this statement as a sign of eternal salvation. Some Christians' erroneous conception of the sins of the cross leads them to share their crosses instead of carrying them. Every negative circumstance, every fall, every suffering is turned into despair and dumped on those around them so they do not have to carry the weight of their cross alone. When these types of people get a disease, they make sure that everyone around them suffers the weight of their cross. Thus, many others are manipulated through this disease. When we see such individuals approaching us, the first thought that comes to mind is that they are bringing us even more trouble with their infinite complaining. Such people will find someone to blame for all the negativity in their life; when this group of people gets together we could nickname them 'the choirs of lamentation.' How many times have we shared a table with a group of whiners and after leaving them, feel drained as though we have been contaminated with the most horrendous diseases?

The silence of the cross is the most important secret in the attainment of both perfect healing and reparation. We should take pain, trials and tribulations and offer them to the Lord instead of giving them away to others. Whenever we share our cross with our neighbor, not only do we waste a treasure of true healing, we also accumulate darkness for our soul because of a lack of charity, love and respect for our neighbor. The silence of the cross invites us into the true silence of the spirit.

Imagination is the greatest contaminator of our intellect. If we silence our imagination we will bring true health to our intellect — the fountain of noble ideas of love. The silence of imagination should be placed in the hands of heaven. Our guardian angel communicates with us through our imagination. The silence of the cross provides us with the greatest treasure of inner peace in the midst of the desert of this painful world.

We must distinguish between sin and sinner. We cannot judge a person who commits adultery; rather, we judge the sinful act of adultery which is the devil. We cannot judge a thief because he is a sinner; we judge the sinful act of theft instead which is Satan. Likewise, rather than judging the sinner (the liar), we judge the sin (the lie) which is Satan. In the same vein we condemn homosexual acts rather than the homosexual which again is the devil himself. When we establish this with clarity, we understand even more the secret of the holy cross because we will be filled with love and charity for our neighbor and therefore charitable to ourselves, submerged in a true ocean of eternal love that emanates from the celestial Father to His creatures.

The growth of my carnal appetite brought serious consequences to my life and to those around me. Sexual impurity is one of the deepest abysses, one of the fastest paths to separate us light years from the presence of God, a path that gravely compromises us with its diabolical realms. I was taken by the Lord to the root of the sins of my ancestors and was shown how I continued multiplying these sins — this horrible curse — for future generations.

The culture into which I was born has exposed man to an unbridled sexual impurity. Early on I began to engage in intense sexual activity with myself. Like the true fallen I fell into the abyss of impurity at the consummation of my first sexual act. Instead of reserving virginity and chastity for sacramental matrimony with its abundance of Christian graces, my ancestors and my culture chose the path of carnal pleasure prior to marriage.

The Lord showed me how that first sexual act submerged me permanently inside the flesh of sin. I entered sexuality through the door of sin. I lost grace and fell back into original sin as if I was never baptized. I received the consequences of all the impurities of my ancestors; therefore, I didn't have any spiritual compass. From that moment on my entire life began to function in the flesh and away from the spirit. My eyes were hungering to penetrate the deepest abyss of sexuality. My eyes were like sponges that would absorb every impregnable detail on the way. Everyone around me stood for sexual versus spiritual values. As a result,

I lost countless graces and the greatest treasure — peace — that we can receive from our neighbors when we are in the state of grace and purity.

I lost my peace through carnal love, a lack of charity, and my non-existent relationship with God. In such a state, the garment of impurity that we carry fills our soul with shame and makes us hide our eyes from God in the same manner as our forefathers did when they fell into original sin. Only through the strictest sacrifices and by acts of true contrition can we return to the grace of purity in our sexuality after we have lost it for years. The sins of the flesh, if not repaired during our earthly life, reveal the most horrible presence of darkness and suffering that separates us from God when we depart this world and present ourselves before the Divine Tribunal.

Atheistic science removed from God has been one of the greatest causes of the loss of many souls. A person who rationalizes his existence and believes that we are a product of evolution has created a world of death and contaminated an immense majority of humanity. Exploiting the spiritual ignorance of humans as if they were puppets is one of the greatest calamities and most sophisticated works of evil. Atheistic science teaches that our sexuality is a physiological need justifying not only homosexuality but also every opening to the unruly desires of the flesh. The Lord told me that sexuality is not a need but a function. A human can survive without a sexual life; By not being sexually active, he may not be able to procreate but surely will not die or be atrophied, physically or emotionally.

The obscure elements of atheistic psychology and all schools of this type of thinking opened one of the biggest gates to hell. They present the human creature in its lowest nature and reduce it to being a simple sexual being cut off from a relationship with the spirit. The Lord says that all of these scientists and those who follow such teachings have brought more death to the world with abortion than all of the wars of humanity from the beginning of time. The sacramental life of matrimony has been lacerated and turned into a mere carnal relationship between humans, bringing consequences of instability, infidelity between relationships and grave promiscuity. Worldwide, millions are born in a state of rejection, directly from the mother's womb. Consequently, instead of coming into the world to be the salt of the earth, they become the fuel of the cruel fire against values and morals in which thousands of souls have been incinerated throughout the history of time. No words can express the tragedy on a spiritual plane of a life driven through the streets of worldly impurity, the repercussions of which lead to a state of cruelty and coldness towards humanity.

It seems as though every sexual and sinful act of pleasure is an internal metamorphosis gradually emptying the human being of all its spiritual existence. This can only lead the soul to a premature death — turning it into a corpse driven by the evil one through the gates of eternal burial. I can relate to being one of these walking corpses. Several years after my encounter with the Lord, I can see today thousands of walking dead people inebriated by impurity heading directly to the abyss of eternal perdition.

It is like witnessing a funeral of corpses walking one after the other into an immense eternal cemetery. We have lost all respect for life. We live in a world of greed inundated with insatiable desires. The Lord showed me how the absence of worldly desire is the presence of Him in us and the abundance of earthly desire is the absence of Him in us. The more attached we are to the world, the less that we are attached to God.

Today, very many souls are lost through greed and inordinate desires. The strongest attachments are human affection, money, power and material possessions. It's like drowning in the middle of the ocean and searching for a rope to cling to that will bring you safely to shore. When we least expect it we find ourselves absolutely externalized, empty of inner life. This is the beginning of the end. A human being without an inner life is like a balloon without air.

Everything we possess has a mouth that has to be fed. If we have a chair we have to find a space for it and maintain it, and so it is with each of our material possessions. If we evaluate the real stature of our spirituality, we have to look around us and assess our possessions, analyzing what we really need and taking note of what is not necessary to keep. We will be surprised to see that most of us are smothered by our material possessions in such a way that we end up enslaved to them. There are people who reach the point of missing opportunities that might improve their life; they cannot mobilize themselves to relocate to a distant place because they cannot take all of their material possessions along. They turn their life into an absurd irony. Being attached to material possessions is bad enough but attachment to human beings is much worse.

Sexual impurity turns the individual into a very insecure person, plunging a very emotionally-unstable person into a grave, nervous crisis filled with immense depression, jealousy, possessiveness, manipulation, maliciousness, cruelty, morbidity and distrust. The typical personality and character of a person infected by an impure life is an immense fear of losing those who give him human affection. These are generally the ones that make that person suffer more and with whom he executes the rudest acts of cruelty. It is as if impurity leads us to hate our own sinful nature and to reject violently everything that represents purity. The same knife that cuts a piece of bread could stab a human being; therefore, it is not the knife (the material instrument) but evil itself and the relationship we have with it.

The true association between human creatures and material creation is the basis of our pure relationship with the Creator. If we are slaves of the material world, we adore creation and not the Creator. We are separated and amputated from grace. The Lord extends His teachings over this particular knowledge in such an abundant way that I would need a few books to narrate this theme in order to be able to preserve the richness in which it was taught to me. He told me that Satan imitates the events of the world in order to deceive us. By examining our human history, we can view the first disguise that Satan deceptively employed on our forefathers, Adam and Even, when he tempted them to eat the forbidden fruit from the tree of good and evil, thereby introducing sin as an alternative way of conduct.

From the instant Satan introduced the adoration of creation, he prevented us from adoring the Creator, who is the very fountain of infinite wisdom. We can carefully observe the influence of this independent thought in our human history. The man who separates himself from God is convinced that the elements of creation will enable him to be self-sufficient from God. Today, more than ever, as we approach the encounter with the final redemption and the closing of this human cycle in relationship with the exiled from paradise, the proposal of the enemy to worship creation couldn't be more attractive and persuasive. What we know today of the New Age Movement is based in this spirit. Every pagan philosophy of the East, every occult metaphysic treaty, all esoteric knowledge, magic, divination, superstition, spiritualism, and astrological charts, lead us to conceive and find self-realization through the powers of nature that is represented with its own spiritual properties.

The Lord explained to me with absolute clarity that nothing in creation has power without the Creator's spirit — neither the moon, sun, stars, planets, nor the plants or the crystals, talismans or amulets. No witch or magician has any power. The last attack from the evil one against humanity began in the 1950s — the last baptism of evil. Paganism has slowly and silently begun to slide into position to invade the heart of western Christianity. The forces of evil prepare this human scenario for one of the greatest and most horrible spectacles that has ever been witnessed in the history of humanity — the idolatry of human beings. Never before has the human being been adored in such a form.

The first great idols were represented through music in the USA and the UK with figures such as Elvis Presley, who very quickly became known as "The King", and the Beatles, in whose presence fans would faint, worshipping the material wealth and power of the rich and famous as displayed in Fortune magazine. Sports heroes, royalty, public servants turned into political celebrities, movie and television actors in general, and high flying bohemians have been turned into models of idol worship for millions of people around the world.

All this is accompanied by the godfather of darkness who does not waste an instant implanting his catechism of hell through the paganism that begins to occupy the principal seat in the living room of all of these stars. One after the other, they begin to declare themselves publicly as believers and followers of these meditation techniques: reincarnation, superstition, divination, the ladder of the seven yogas and all the other forms that I mentioned previously. The astuteness of the evil one is so great and his strategy so subliminal that to condemn or denounce any of these practices in these times, even in Christian gatherings, can be a reason for scorn, persecution or great discrimination.

Great masses of people and a majority of Christians have been taken in by this wave of spiritual darkness, led away from Christ-centeredness into an incredibly profound abyss of illusion; being convinced by the enemy that they have achieved the light since the greatest trick of the devil is disguising himself as an angel of light. Every pagan philosophy, metaphysical treaty of the occult, esoterical orientation and all seven schools of yoga speak of love, of the renunciation of the material in order to achieve universal harmony. They present a picture of love, a hard concept to resist for those who are trapped by a weak faith and on a path of sin. All these beautiful teachings lead the individual to believe that in the end all of us are God.

Many people born in the 1950s were accompanied in their cribs by immense crystals and ruled by astrological charts and tarot readings, according to the pagan practices of their parents. Many of them were baptized with names of stars from the magicians. Millions were received as reincarnated beings with a determined destiny. Many grew in the midst of the slavery of numerology or mystic Kabbalah. So they live in this world separated from God, penetrating deeper and deeper into paganism, thereby distancing themselves even further from the spiritual light.

What is the evil one planning by amputating so severely our Christian life? Is it to steal the weapons that we have received through generations of Christianity along with so many blessings? Previous generations led rich spiritual lives leaving future generations an immense testimony of life in the spirit of God. Without those same weapons, we cannot defend ourselves and we cannot protect our children from the snares of the devil. Left vulnerable, we will have difficulties facing all the events that are to come over humanity. The Lord urgently wants to use our arms, lips, mind and heart to speak about the plan of salvation. It is our physical property, this material, human body, the actual temple in which our Lord is manifesting Himself. We are called to return to the house of God, to break down all the false idols and to learn how to worship Him again so that He can restore us and give us back the weapons we have lost while we were growing and adoring creation, searching for our own glory in the midst of the deceiving enemy.

The calling is to strip ourselves of all corruption so that we can clean the temple of God in us, to stop it from being the latrine of Satan, to return to the original grace that we received through baptism, and if we haven't been baptized, to receive that holy baptism in Christ our Lord thereby discovering the true path, the absolute truth, which is eternal life. The Lord spoke and showed me a very sad picture of my soul, a desolate territory of sin that had accumulated over many years of my life while walking in absolute obscurity, each step which gradually led me to death. Simultaneously, He showed me the grace of His infinite mercy, His endless love.

At the time of my encounter with the Lord I didn't know that I would return to this material world. It was the last thing that occurred to me. He was taking me through these experiences as though it was my personal judgment. Today I understand why. It makes sense that after going through the personal judgment, I can still be here many years later writing this. At the same time, I suffer the limitations of human language to express divine revelation. I trust the Holy Spirit will complete in the heart of the reader the richness of this infused knowledge that I am not able to present in the purity in which it was received. I don't doubt at all that the Lord in His infinite wisdom wanted me to live this experience so that I could be one more witness of His glory, not because I am special and not because I have received any special privileges — unique or distinct — but because the Lord wants to show us how He glorifies Himself more in our misery than in our merits. By choosing a sinner as the mouthpiece of His grace, He invites us to trust in His mercy rather than the merits for which we search as we strive to get closer to Him.

Rescuing me from Satan's pits of destruction is a clear example of how much He glorifies Himself in the sinner in order to redeem and free us from the strangulating hands of the enemy — sin itself. To trust, believe and live for Jesus and receive Him in our hearts so that we can never let Him go is what I received in these teachings from my Divine master. The state I was in during the teachings He gave me through the presence of His voice is very difficult to describe. While He was talking to me, I saw what He was referring to. The only way to express it in words would be to say that everything He spoke about materialized in front of my eyes.

To acknowledge that we are inhabited in the human body with flesh that is the product of sin is of extreme importance for the spiritual realization of the individual. If we are the product of original sin, this makes us indirect partners of the one who caused this falling, as in the case of a woman deceived by a man who only wants to use her for his sexual appetite and leaves her pregnant and then disappears from her life, leaving a great part of himself inside of her. It doesn't matter which way you put it; that man is the father of that child. There is no escaping that reality. The same thing occurs with us through sin.

Through our forefathers we enter into a relationship with the evil one and it doesn't matter how we characterize it; he is the father of the sin of the flesh. Because of him we were born in a very painful way through Eve in order to die in even greater pain. We have to assume this reality in concrete terms; otherwise, we would never understand our weaknesses, misery, fragility, vulnerability and the evil that is in us because of our ancestral nature. Understanding this leads us into a real union with the spirit. The permanent communion between body and soul are essential to union with God.

If we have no love for our flesh, the world offers us nothing. The evil one has no way of perverting us if we are detached from our physical self. The flesh turns into our worst enemy if we do not recognize it in our sinful nature. Being armed with this knowledge, we can begin training our physical body in the same way a horse is trained. The spirit is the rider and the body is the horse. When we know the nature of this animal, we are able to have it under our control and discipline. A horse with a rider is a useful element of labor, a vehicle that facilitates the movement of innumerable duties. At that moment we are facilitating the grace of God so that He can inhabit our body because it will be the true temple of the Holy Spirit. When we subject the flesh to the strict obedience of the Holy Spirit, we will find that the Holy Spirit will be the one riding this instrument. The Lord will dwell within us and we will dwell within Him. It entails integrating ourselves with our good nature, while sustaining the reins of our bad nature with both hands until the moment we deposit our vehicle into the grave and elevate ourselves to the celestial realm, free from the corruption of the flesh.

We live in a transitory world that will pass by faster than we think. The Lord showed me this material world and I could see it as a very small instant in eternity. In this small instant thousands of souls were being wasted, blinded and wandering, certain that they were fighting to conquer something real and permanent. It is sad to see so many people trapped in all the techniques of self-realization of personal growth that supposedly leads them to achieve any goal in their lives with the belief that they, by their own means, are able to achieve anything they want to achieve. Positive thinking and all the incredible traps of self-esteem, a product of the atheistic science of the New Age, is the darkness that has deified man to the point of convincing him that he has absolute control over himself. It saddens me even more to see how all these errors have penetrated our Church. I discovered, through the grace of Christ, that many priests, religious, and laity have adopted methods of eastern meditation, Da Silva methods, the enneagram, the theology of liberation and so many other dark elements that have turned some areas of our Church into a scenario of spiritual decadence, contaminated with the most absurd intellectual stubbornness. The worst error a human being can commit on the path to spiritual perfection is to feed the intelligence before subjecting himself to the divine wisdom of the word of the Lord.

There is nothing worse in our Church than an intelligent, cultured priest, of distinguished class and impressive style, educated in the finest universities of the world, who does not have the presence of the spirit of the Lord, which does not dwell in an edifice of such pretension. I am not suggesting that we condemn education, culture or human dignity, but I do believe that one cannot begin to build an edifice starting at the top. If in the formation of seminarians (as I have unfortunately discovered) more attention is placed on the intellectual, philosophical and theological education than the spiritual growth of the seminarian in his relationship with God, the discipline of the flesh and the orientation towards the mystical presence of the body of Jesus, then unfortunately we are forming priests, religious and laity for the world and not for the glory of God.

If it is true that it is in the world that priests are going to serve the Lord, it is also true that all the knowledge received during this religious formation is not to be used to accommodate the world but to present the justice, mercy and laws of God in order to believe the gospel. Above all, to characterize the circumstances that humanity could face in any given time of history. The truth taught by Our Lord Jesus Christ is singular, eternal and not subject to revision. Taking the present scenario into consideration, we can certainly understand the message of darkness with clarity by scrutinizing the occult sciences, eastern pagan beliefs, scientific proposals of self-realization and all other areas that I have already mentioned.

Why has all the practices of the New Age been propagated so highly within the last 70 years? Not only has evil spread, it has caused millions of souls to lapse into spiritual darkness; entire generations of Christians have thus turned into pagans within the period of a few decades. It is very clear that the intention of the evil one is to lead human beings to a primitive spiritual state, taking them back to a period three or four thousand years before Christ, when hope of redemption was far from reach. Instead of giving man the grace of 2,000 years of accumulated wisdom obtained after the resurrection of Our Lord, evil has lead humanity to a state of spiritual regression. It is therefore not surprising that man has become decadent, intensely glorifying and idolizing himself.

It follows that sexual impurity has reached levels more degenerate than those of Sodom and Gomorrah, Babylon and the Roman Empire. Violence has been industrialized. Abortion crimes have increased. The persecution of purity has turned into a slogan of fashion. The Church is a target for comedians. Religious life is described as a model of fanaticism. This proves that at this present time in our lives we are receiving signals, announced by the prophets from the past, that have debilitated the spiritual base reaching so many generations of Christians who were always saved by Jesus — the ruin of so many souls at the most critical moment of history where man is called with urgency to renew his relationship with God. My experience with the voice of the Lord is quite extensive. I could write more concerning this part of my vision but I find that I have to come to terms with myself as to where I should stop and continue with the second stage of this experience.

Encounter with the Lord's Image and Person

As I was looking around, trying to discover where the voice of the Lord was coming from, I found myself submerged up to my waist in a small lake of crystal water. I was looking up with my arms outstretched and found myself in three different states: in the room with the bats, in the lake, and lying down on the grass with the voice of the Lord speaking to me as He led me through the most extensive teaching on my life, humanity, our relationship between good and evil, and all that I have thus far narrated.

Besides being acutely conscious of my presence in the three different states, I was also keenly aware of the relationship between each. I know that this will seem just as inconceivable to you as it seemed to me. I cannot even touch the surface of perfection, peace and absolute wisdom in which all this took place. As I looked up, my attention was focused on the lake. I felt the presence around me of an immense and precious golden rock, something impossible to describe. It seemed to be as big as the

universe. While unimaginable in size, my human
intellect could still fathom it. I could perceive
something even greater in this grand apparition.
Even though my heart felt the presence of the Lord,
I wanted to disappear into the lake. Yet, as I focused
on the pinnacle of the rock, His incredible
transparent and majestic goodness gave me
strength. I totally melted in His presence. No words
can describe my encounter with our King. His aura
penetrated me completely as if I was united to Him.

The first incident I can describe of my encounter is
the manifestation of the Holy Spirit through whom I
received my baptism. The Holy Spirit enabled me to
fully comprehend everything that I experienced.
Receiving the blessing of the Holy Spirit at baptism,
and the opportunity to cultivate an ongoing personal
relationship with God is the greatest gift that one
can receive. If we could only appreciate the
importance of the anointing of the Holy Spirit first
received in baptism. By this gift, we receive the
grace to know perfection, the perfect existence of
heaven, the existence of purgatory and hell, and our
relationship between good and evil.

When the soul faces the tribunal of our Lord as I
did, it will find nothing that is unknown. Everything
has been infused in us through the workings of the
Holy Spirit. It is sin that has caused this wisdom to
lie dormant in us and leads us to separate ourselves
from grace. The soul knows everything in the

presence of the Lord. The only confusion the soul encounters at the moment of being stripped of the flesh or physical death is the encounter with its relationship with evil. This takes the soul by surprise because it never imagined how far it was separated from God and how the relationship with the Holy Spirit was damaged. There is no way to repair the immense pain at the moment of Divine Justice.

I saw the Divine Presence immersed in majestic light. At the same time, the most beautiful spectrum of colors as could delight the eyes appeared. They seemed to be as living creatures because of the enormous animation in which they existed. There is no comparison between the light and the colors I saw and what we see in the material world. In the midst of the transparency in which the Lord was appearing to me, the light and colors were presenting Him in a different light. His hair was shoulder length and appeared in various shades of gold from the darkest to the lightest. When I looked at the face of the Lord I submerged myself completely in His eyes, which embodied the most infinite love and compassion. They changed from yellow to blue to green, colors that caressed, all the while bringing the greatest relief that a soul could desire. To see the eyes of Jesus is to find the absolute realization of a spiritual existence. There was nothing I would ever wish to see more than His precious eyes. In Him lies absolute plenitude.

A soul in the earthly life searching for personal fulfillment can only find it in the eyes of the Lord. Only He can satiate the soul that is thirsting for the light. During our earthly life we all face difficult tests and trials; sometimes this is caused by not being in the state of grace because of sin. So often human beings waste their life absurdly searching for material happiness that is not only impossible to find, but also a cruel trap of the enemy to distract them from the true fountain of eternal happiness. Some look for the philosophical stone while others try to fill that void by accumulating fortunes. Still others resort to human affections (sexuality). Some undertake the most daring adventures but when all is said and done we can see that the myriad of different ways and alternatives offered by the world only lead us on the path to the most absurd perdition. This is because nothing and no one can bring us true happiness, only He who created us.

While gazing at the Lord I could actually see heaven. Our Lord (the Divine Presence) was the resplendent mansion through which I could see great numbers of angels and saints. No words can adequately describe the face of Our Lord — an eternally young, wise, powerful, merciful face, filled with the most infinite love, placed in an existence free of time, age and space. I would have expected to see Him dressed in a tunic but I can only say that He was dressed in the most precious light. At the moment Our Lord first manifested

Himself in the rock, I felt an immense necessity to dive and cover my eyes, to hide my entire existence from such a majestic presence, but He firmly held me, preventing my escape. He deeply penetrated my consciousness, allowed me to contemplate the most precious experience that any living creature can ever experience.

I could fathom the presence of all the celestial creatures knowing the immaculate perfection of the hierarchical law in which all divine existence cohabitates in His creation. Even if I had been taught by the wisest and holiest of men, I would never have imagined that the celestial order could live in the midst of such a strict and majestic hierarchy. I also saw and could comprehend the angelic choirs and the redemption of the human being taken to the level of eternal glory, having achieved the state of holiness. I also saw the most splendid of all human creatures, the Blessed Virgin Mary. As she emerged from the midst of the most colorful light, she presented herself as if she was coming from the very womb of all the angels and saints. She was filled with the most precious grace and humility. Feeling the deepest maternal emptiness that existed in my soul until that very moment, I saw all of them praising and worshipping the Lord in a single choir which cannot be described in human terms. The presence of such perfection can only produce the state of permanent ecstasy. A veil of holy submission centered on the Virgin Mary enveloped the union of the spirit. The presence of our celestial Mother covers all the angelical choirs and saints under a single mantle of love and seems to consume everything in His fire of divine love when presented before the celestial King.

It is hard to imagine, with the limitations of our rationality, a specific order containing a spiritual plane that is invisible to our human consciousness. All the creatures that I mentioned were attuned to the presence of the Lord. In His divinity, heaven was melting and from Him emanated all these marvelous creatures in countless numbers, as though everything existed in His interior and He was being unveiled with the most indescribable splendor. Our Lady, the Virgin Mary, centered my relationship with the Lord with immense tenderness. It seemed as though I was united to her through a spiritual umbilical cord through which all the impulses of my heart were given perfectly to Our Lord, and while in her womb preparing to be born, began to look at the unveiling of a life never dreamt of. At the same time, it was immensely sad to experience the celestial life while still being attached to this earthly existence. All the while, I couldn't avoid being conscious of my body which was tied up in that dark room filled with bats.

To find out through my celestial Mother that I have lived a motherless life for 47 years, turning down the most precious gift — the most magnificent alliance of love between Jesus and Mary — was painful, sad and devastating. The power of God is so immense that a creature such as I can only melt before His Supreme Majesty. Despite the pain of knowing how obscure my relationship has been with Him, when I encountered the multitude of angels and saints, I discovered my association with each one of them with absolute perfection, without any effort, and in the midst of the most natural beauty.

Further on, I will clarify my relationship with each group of angels, saints and the Virgin Mary because every instant of our lives is connected one way or another with all the celestial realms. I will also describe the relationship with the fallen angels (demons) and condemned souls who, until the last instant of our earthly life, influence our activities (even if we are in a state of grace), in the hope of ensnaring us.

My knowledge of Jesus and Mary was so poor that every discovery was a profound one. I never learned catechism or paid attention to my religious classes. To top it off, I left the Church when I was 14 years old. No matter how well versed a person may be in doctrine, he will not have the slightest idea of the immensity of the mystery of His incarnation or of the sacred relationship we have with Our Lady, the Virgin Mary, or of our close connection with the angels and saints if he has not experienced a personal encounter with Jesus. The knowledge of God would be as sterile as the lives of the Sanhedrin during the public life of Jesus. That is why, in these end times as we prepare for the second coming of the Lord, we are going through spiritual bankruptcy in our Church. In spite of it all, the Holy Spirit continuously renews the life of the faithful hearts from east to west and from north to south.

No matter how much we study the deep mysteries in the Sacred Scriptures or perfect the deposit of theological knowledge, if we do not have the presence of love profoundly in our heart we will never savor even a minimal drop of the absolutely pure divine essence — an infinite ocean of love above all knowledge. The many avenues revealed by God to His creatures combined with the abundance of written wisdom constitute a spiritual richness destined to lead us closer to His immeasurable love. That is why if we direct all our human existence towards that divine love, we will be purified and elevated to the most immense glory even if we are spiritually illiterate. An encounter with Jesus does not have to be achieved by a painful experience or like my kidnapping. We can achieve it by searching for true abandonment in God who awaits that moment from His creature with immense love.

The Charismatic renewal in our Church is a great show of mercy from Our Lord. The Holy Spirit is as present today as in the holy cenacle of Pentecost but we have to find God in our own way. We have to use our own resources to open our own hearts and run in search of Him. We must embrace ourselves now using all the weapons that He has given to us as a just Father who only feeds with love the prodigal son. His love will never cease. He knows the misery and darkness that lies in our human nature. That is why He has the most immense compassion.

I was staring at the Lord with the most profound sadness that seemed to take the bottom of my heart from a surface of fire. I asked Him why I always ended up doing the evil I didn't want to do. The Lord showed me the intimate relationship that we have with good and evil from the very first moment we are born until the last instant of life. The tremendous fight between the flesh that wants to dwell in sin and the soul that desires so much to elevate itself towards God instills in us the importance of recognizing the sinful nature of the flesh and the good nature of the spirit. The more we recognize this factor of our human existence, the more attention that can be given to the strengthening of our soul as a sure path of absolute dominion over the flesh. That is why I always ended up doing the bad I didn't want to do because I had no control over my flesh. I was a slave to the flesh and was guided by instincts and sexuality in all of my actions. God doesn't test anyone. We bring the trials and tribulations on ourselves because of our sins and the prosecutor of that test is the fountain of all sin. The discipline or mortification of our lower nature, the flesh, has a purifying effect on our flesh, turning it into the temple of the Holy Spirit.

In the presence of the Lord, it was painful for the soul to witness or to acknowledge its utter former oblivion to the abundant graces present while in a perpetual state of sin. The Lord revealed to me why I always ended up doing the wrong thing when I was really trying to do good. He showed me my angry soul. It was in a cold and tormented prison while my bad nature was enjoying a moment of pleasure that was only contributing towards pushing me down one more step into the darkness. It was a macabre reality.

I also saw the eyes of those who had sinned with me. They were going through an interior anguish with the exception of those who seemed to be consumed by the darkness: the prostitutes standing on the corner on a cold, lonely night, the tormented eyes of a masked bank robber, the fearful eyes of a girl lying to her teacher, the eyes of the priest who elevates the Eucharist with corrupted hands because of sin, dying inside as a result of betraying the promise made to his Lord; faces that we sometimes see in a tortuous duality that consumes, corrupts and withers human nature — a product of original sin.

In the midst of all this pain, the Lord showed me that He is always there in all these actions, no matter how dark, to alleviate the weight of sin from the shoulders of our tormented souls that recognize something is totally wrong. I speak of the soul that is separated from God as I was at the moment He called me. A soul that dwells within the holy territory of its Creator walks healthily, freely and at peace in the midst of the most macabre routes of human exile. Withholding love, a heart separated from God carries a load that could make great titans cry a river of tears. It is an endless lesson involving every aspect of our lives.

The Lord provides the strength necessary to overcome our ancestral difficulties with divine perfection. He has done so with the saints, allowing them to go through great torments with their animal nature in order to purify them of everything that He knows should be cleansed in spite of the temporal torments. He knows how transitory our suffering is and how terrible it will be to be purified after our earthly life. The mercy of God is immeasurable. It doesn't have borders or preferences; He loves His creatures.

I can testify to His infinite love, an immense love that would calcify our existence if we would receive it all at once. That is why the mystery of the nearness to God is gradually unfolded and why He brings His creatures into His arms dispensing His love little by little like a drop of water that trickles towards the sun and ends up evaporating before the incandescence of the heat by fusing itself in its rays.

In the midst of my anguish, His eyes presented me with a single instant of my life, allowing me to see how I ended up doing that which I most detested. I saw how a human creature by nature hates sin. The more sins that are committed, the more torment that exists and the more desolation the person seeks in search of lost happiness. I could see how in the midst of my most intense sinful activity (when I thought I had enjoyed the most physically), my soul was bleeding rivers of internal pain that consumed my entire being. My eyes seemed like lanterns of sadness covered in makeup like those of a carnival clown, a hungry clown that laughs and yells in the midst of poverty looking for a piece of bread to satisfy his hunger. The macabre scenario could only be seen by the soul with such clarity while being taken by the hand of the Lord who was able to repair this for all humanity. Only in Him will we be able to face the absurd misery of our human existence because with His support we will transcend to the divine and find sense in our suffering and pain.

Why did I do the wrong I didn't want to do? Why didn't I feed my soul and have strength to face my own animal nature? Why was I consuming only the error of my passions and why have I never breathed the pure air of the spirit that liberates and heals? Why were my eyes not fixed on Jesus but only on my iniquities and me? The Lord showed me intergenerational inheritance, the strong force that binds those who walk in sin, who walk over the territory of evil. In addition to suffering the consequences of our own sins, we also carry additional baggage —the sins of our ancestors.

Why do we do the wrong we don't want to do? Because if we live in sin we are open to an extensive path of consequences over a territory of evil whose laws do not forgive and do not let go any opportunity to seduce us in falling deeper into darkness.

While in the flesh, the soul falls into evil ways and begins to receive the accumulated account of past actions resulting in possible eternal condemnation or a severe life in purgatory. It is like arriving at the hometown of hundreds of past generations and identifying ourselves as those responsible for all pending accounts. These accounts are to be collected none other than by the administrator, jailer, prince of this world — Satan himself.

Only God knows the consequences of the state of the soul. He who continuously lives in sin walks over an old accumulated debt and his temporary earthly life will not suffice to repay what was contracted by many other relatives no longer alive. The most obvious result is that he will end up as one more cadaver walking towards his own eternal burial, consumed under the weight of his accumulated debt.

Even though this teaching of the Lord may appear harsh and difficult, I find that to live in grace in God's grace is like wearing the diver's rubber suit to swim through the deep waters of this material world, carrying on our shoulders the oxygen tank which will not run empty if it is connected to the eternal fountain: Jesus Christ. On the contrary, to live a sinful life bereft of grace is to not only lose everything spiritually but to pass on an even greater debt to future generations. To inherit money, fame and power from ancestors can lead our souls on the road to perdition. The power accumulated by a fortune obtained through evil ways is so dark that it is plagued by demons that are in control of every cent of such wealth under strict supervision by the devil. It is also true that all this can be turned into blessings for humanity and for the glory of God if used properly. However, the percentage of people who will act in the right way is so small that it is hardly noticeable. Jesus tells us in regards to this matter, "It is easier for a camel to pass through the eye of a needle than for a rich man to enter into the kingdom of Heaven."

The evil one keeps a perfect account of our soul. Every debt contracted by him will be charged by removing light from our souls. The Lord Jesus is by no means condemning fame or power. He is only pointing out the abyss that lays parallel to each step of our earthly life.

The Lord wants us to live an abundant life filled with dignity, enriched with a good reputation and a favorable testimony of our life from our neighbor. If only we would keep our eyes on Him — the Creator — and enjoy the gifts of His creation instead of adoring them, we could lead a good and happy life.

The reason why we find ourselves filled with darkness at times is because the evil one has established a great battle against our inner peace, unceasingly detonating charges of anxiety, intolerance, uneasiness, etc. All of this will affect our relationship with God and the reception of His graces because we would be unplugging ourselves from the eternal fountain of God's joy and peace, as well as physical and spiritual health. Every time we find ourselves lacking inner peace, it is because the evil one has been attacking us one way or another.

The soul's crossing from the path of darkness of this earthly life into eternity is beyond our comprehension or intellectual belief. At the moment of standing before the Lord no longer on the material level, everything that takes place is outside of any possible rational explanation. The only way to relay this knowledge will be whatever the Lord will permit to filter through within a simple language strictly related to the battle between good and evil and the weapons that have been given to us in order to survive.

Interpenetrated in the Lord, I'm made perfectly aware of all my entire earthly life in the territory of good and evil. Our relationship with the forces of good and evil so much determines our account before the Lord that we must keep strict vigilance over our actions so that the numbers won't multiply on the wrong territory, invariably exposing our souls to grave danger of damnation.

I call it 'the account' only to be able to present a practical and rational way to illustrate that there is not a single action of our lives that will not escape the eyes of our Lord Jesus. The redemption we have been given by God the Father through His Son, Jesus Christ, is so large that through His merits we are capable of paying every single debt against us with His blood. It is possible then not only to pay off all of our existing debts with His blood, but also to repay the consequences inflicted by them, as long as we do it while we are still living in the flesh in this material world.

Everything that has been damaged in the flesh due to the consequences of sin has to be repaired in that very flesh. If we are able to do this reparation while in the flesh we will be spiritually free. The only way is to place it before the foot of the cross of Jesus, asking Him to cover all of that walk on the path of darkness with His blood, so that it may never again be counted against us before His holy tribunal. The Lord Jesus led me to walk through the actions of my past before Him; I relived it even though I was averse to viewing it.

In each one of my experiences I went through the same situation. At the end, an enormous emptiness enveloped me that increased the silent fury within, filling me with uncertainty, putting down the weapons of the spirit, allowing my instincts and passions to govern, creating a cruel and inscrutable loneliness combined with an apparent lusty joy imposing a false happiness. It seemed that the more my flesh was winning under its onerous weight, the more I was losing the desire to be pure, good, forgiving and virtuous.

Today, I clearly see the souls of the people who are trapped in the world of passion. It is like observing a prisoner dragging his chains in the midst of a smiling carnival, filled with the apparent joy that binds the prisoner of darkness. Exhausted faces infused in pleasure, insensitive to tenderness, indifferent to true love, hardened by walking thousands of miles on the enemy's territory. The existential pain caused by that intimate relationship with evil turns the human creature unconsciously into a promoter of his own misery.

As the old saying goes, "misery loves company." As the sick man conceals his promiscuity, he contaminates a great number of people by doing nothing to avoid it as if wanting to find company in his own disintegration. It's the poison of evil that he wants to transmit to everyone. It is a poison that accumulates into a great deposit in our organism until it turns into the little bag of the serpent's poison that attacks and inoculates without piety. We see a defense mechanism of the same darkness in the marching of homosexuals in the summer, promoting the poison of promiscuity in which they are prisoners. They feel a need to share it with the whole world, raising high the flag of sin from the highest mountain.

What an enormous discovery for the soul to perceive the true existence of eternal life. No matter how much one tries to believe, the most difficult time in our journey through life is when we have doubts, regardless of how great our faith seems to be. To be in the presence of such an immense wonder is to finally realize, when we are standing firmly in eternity, how we walked through life and never truly comprehended it because we were attached intimately to our mortality. To realize eternity is like waking up in the midst of the most marvelous dream, knowing that it will never end.

If we could truly believe with our heart, mind and soul that each action in our earthly life bears eternal consequences, then everything would cease to die in and around us. Life would take on another meaning because then the decadence of our flesh through biological aging would turn into joy knowing that we are closer and closer to the eternal communion with God, free from the prison of our flesh. Our dreams would not die, our family would not die, our friends would never disappear, and our hope would never diminish if we became aware that the death of the flesh is only the passing through to a superior state. There, life reigns in the midst of the Creator where the greatest joy is felt by accepting Jesus and recognizing that one has already been saved and the path to eternal glory has already been constructed with His blood. This was clarified when I asked the Lord about the terrible chain we create by committing evil when not wanting to do so.

My Own Trial

In the midst of this lesson the Lord led me to a personal judgment where my contemplative state ended as well as the information He gave me. The romance between heaven and me suddenly transformed into a scenario of my life or, shall I say, the threat of eternal death to my soul. I was standing in the territory of the evil one gazing towards heaven. This alone revealed the state of my soul: 33 years of mortal sin. These were years in which I believed only in everything that would benefit me and myself and nothing else, resulting in a severe separation from God.

There is no half way before the Holy Tribunal. You can't say we were sort of good or sort of bad. The dividing line disappears and we are left either on one side or the other. I stood on evil ground. The devil had been my master and on his terrain I was to render an account to my Lord. The state of my soul represented a poor human sinner, similar to that of a husband whose wife caught him in his lover's bed. What else can he do to render an account of such an act other than to acknowledge it and hope for mercy and forgiveness from his wife? This is the way I found myself in the presence of the Lord: unfaithful in the midst of my sins and in bed with the evil one for many years.

From the moment that my judgment began, I could not look at the Lord. I didn't have the strength to contemplate the beauty of such love while He showed me the most hidden corners of my earthly life. I was conscious of the water that I found myself in. I couldn't tell if the water was giving me a sensation of warmth or coldness. Even though I was enveloped in nature, within all the earthly elements, the fact that I was living in the spirit transformed my sense of perception. I was covered with an overwhelming sadness surrounded by abominable creatures beyond my wildest dreams and imagination. I saw how the Lord allowed me to begin the encounter with the true state of my soul, now that I knew the difference between a good relationship with Him and a relationship with impurity.

Heaven communicated to me through my own pedagogy, symbolism, and language. There was nothing in the communication with our Lord that was unfamiliar to any knowledge that I had acquired in the world. It was a perfect communication. In my view, the devils resembled human beings. They were the most abominable creatures that one could imagine. I understood that these infernal creatures manifested themselves according to our relationship to them. If a Japanese man is before the Lord's tribunal, that evil will surely reveal itself according to the Japanese culture. This does not cease to prove the fact that the devils are angelical creatures and that in that final instant they are unveiling their presence in the highest state, which is the absolute, critical moment to conquer the fallen soul eternally.

If we knew with clarity that we were standing in the territory of sin, we would never allow ourselves to be deceived or manipulated and turned into such absurd puppets of Satan. At that moment I perceived the most excruciating pain of my whole human existence. It felt as though my soul was stolen, raped and trampled on. The worst part was recognizing that I had voluntarily caused this. Even though the word 'rape' might sound exaggerated, I truly sensed a violation in the inner recesses of my soul. I could see the different angles in which evil worked in me and how it invaded the spaces of my inner life, gradually releasing the minutest details of the presence of God within. The first thing the devil does to a creature that lives in his territory is to strip him of what he hates the most — everything that we inwardly possess through the Holy Spirit.

The reason why Satan hates us is because we have been created in the image and likeness of God and he despises God the most. It is extremely frightening to contemplate the enormous power our enemy has over us when we fall within his grasp.

He leads us to believe that we are standing on firm ground, selling us lies instead of truth, illusion instead of reality. That's the way his influence begins in our earthly life. When we have been removed from the center of gravity in our spiritual life, we are outside the heart of Jesus.

The Role of Evil Forces in Our Lives

I found myself in evil territory with a clear picture of how my entire life was gradually taken to an abyss by souls filled with perpetual sadness. I understood that the goal of all this diabolical manipulation during my entire earthly life was to separate me completely from God and lead me to spiritual death. I saw how the fallen angels of heaven, of pure intellect, conceived the incarnation of God as man before it happened. When they saw Christ conceived by the power of the Holy Spirit through a humble woman — the holy Virgin Mary — they rebelled and refused to obey and serve the human creature, the man-God, the Christ who was to be incarnated. From that moment on the battle was established with the angels. By being thrown out of heaven, they turned from light into darkness and were separated from the light at the beginning of creation. The fallen angels knew that man would occupy the spaces they lost in heaven. The angels fell from the nine choirs, making way for the formation of saints as their replacement. When we observe the saints' lives we can distinguish how God has formed the state of sanctity in accordance with the angelic choirs in which the saint is illuminated and from which direction he receives spiritual guidance.

Our forefathers were stripped of original grace by these fallen angels who made them lose their original innocence and sold creation as a fountain of nourishment, tempting man to fix his eyes on evil, thereby removing his eyes from the Creator, leaving them in a state in which the fallen angels were found when they rebelled against the celestial Father. The rebel angels were exiled and thrown out of paradise along with man, thus placing humanity in the same realm as the fallen angels. Since man rebelled against God due to an angel (Satan) that considered himself superior to Him, when throwing man out of paradise, God carried out perfect justice, distinguishing human sin from the sin of the angels and giving human creatures the opportunity to return to paradise through the purification of his soul, which was created in the image and likeness of God. It is necessary for the soul to experience exile, in order to conquer the separation between life in the flesh and the return to paradise. Man experiences great difficulty in trying to defend himself from the snares of the fallen angels who do all they can to destroy the purity of soul in human creatures, thereby keeping them from occupying the places that were prepared for them in heaven.

We pay for this original association with Satan by walking in his territory as though being married to the enemy, which is this material world. Our entire life is based on divorcing ourselves from that reality by rebuking the relationship that we contracted due to the devil's temptation of Adam and Eve and the ensuing original sin committed by our original ancestors. We have to make a firm decision either to love God only or to confirm our matrimonial past with the prince and administrator of this material world — Satan — through living an existence completely nourished by the world and the flesh. When man was thrown out of paradise he was subjected to his mortal nature through the flesh, which can be seen by the difficulties he experiences during his exile on earth. Within the human creature lives a wise soul that suffers the imprisonment of the flesh, continually aims towards God and rebukes the vulnerability and misery of evil. The devil, well aware of the mortal nature of the flesh of man and its origin, controls it as he pleases because the soul has not divorced itself from personal and original sin.

Even when the soul decides to divorce the devil, the devil will still relentlessly continue to ensnare it until the last breath of its earthly life. Depending on the spiritual state in which the soul finds itself at the moment of death, the devil might continue tormenting it until the last moment of freedom from all attachments to earthly life. Every instant of our life, whether we are engaged in goodness or evil, is present in eternity. That is why our acts are clearly marked on the side of good or evil.

If we really understood the importance of heaven, we would be aware of the body, soul, mind and the invisible spirits surrounding us; however, we are deaf, mute and blind to the divine spirits because of the presence of the flesh that influences our lives in a definitive way. We would also recognize the spiritual warfare that we find ourselves in from the moment we are born into this exile on earth.

Man inhabited the earth thousands of years before Christ arrived and before He established His kingdom in our midst. During the period of time before the redemption, humanity lived in the hands of the devil, in a spiritual state which in general terms was more attached to paganism than to a true relationship with God because of the lack of grace. In other words, it was the price that had to be paid because of original sin. Over the ages God has gradually drawn closer to man through his prophets and prepared man for his return to paradise in the midst of some of the most painful lessons. God spoke of the chosen people, the Israelites. We heard about the twelve tribes of Israel. This specific group, referred to in the scriptures, is the result of thousands of years of teaching by the Creator to His creatures.

After leading humanity through the long periods of divine absence God returned, taught one more lesson, and picked the human fruits of His lessons every time until He created the group called the 'chosen ones.' After establishing His covenant with our father, Abraham, God continued His covenant with Moses, who gave us the Ten Commandments. Throughout history, God has always picked His chosen ones and led them along the path of righteousness, equipping them in their battle against the enemy. Finally, God provided His people with specific rules to live by. This, in turn, prepared mankind for the coming of Christ, our Redeemer and Savior, culminating in the forgiveness of our sins and the reopening of the gates of heaven. Up to this time, earthly life was an ardent, long and painful prison for humanity. The devil reigned over humanity for many years. In spite of being born with the knowledge of the holy Decalogue (Ten Commandments), man was separated from it through sin and turned into a slave of the law itself. As the prince of this world, Satan will maintain his influence over all souls until the return of the Lord, who will banish the devil forever when the New Jerusalem shines among us.

It is difficult, if not impossible, to explain in human terms how intimacy with evil can become a part of our life. The best way to describe what I have seen through the eyes of my spirit is that an evil force of various dimensions generates everything. When we are in mortal sin and walking in evil territory, it is as though we are gradually weaving a great web until the moment we become trapped in it, immobilized and separated from any possible help in the human realm. Only the grace of God can break these attachments generated by our own evil acts when we become intimate with evil. This does not take into account the evil acts which we inherited from our ancestors that augment gravely the weaving of these attachments.

For instance, if we visualize the scene of greed, I can tell you that the forces of darkness feed this greed with unimaginable intensity because that sin is the fountain of many others. Even if minor sins were committed, it is inevitable that they will develop into more sinful ones from which man will be able to free himself only through the grace of God. The devil will be in charge of promoting this greed at all costs. When we live in the territory of evil, the devil reigns in our imagination and fills it with the necessary elements to produce the primal nature of a particular sin. Being an angel, he is by nature superior to us, having pure intellect and full knowledge of all our inclinations because he is the owner and creator of them. Being free from time and space, he knows what the sinner wants before the sinner does.

When the devil captures us, he runs our emotions, instincts and sexuality, thereby greatly influencing our lives and leaving us very little space to feel conscious of the chain that begins to grasp our souls as his grip gradually tightens. We are talking about souls without God, completely separated from grace. When living in this state, we cannot see that we have acquired the mannerisms and behavior typical of the group of sins in which our relationship with evil is centered. The person in an ongoing state of mortal sin displays a behavioral pattern based on the type of sin committed that his master infuses in him. The type of sin committed determines the characteristics of the demons he has for companions.

It is easy for a person who stands firmly on holy ground to clearly see when someone is controlled by a determined group of sins that typically reunite a legion of evil spirits intent on manipulating a series of activities typical of those particular types of sin. That's why we have saints who know us, are able to read our souls, and are capable of seeing the type of atmosphere that surrounds us and can accurately label the type of sin committed. When such a person undergoes a conversion after receiving the grace of God (the only way one can achieve it), he is not aware of his involvement with the darkness that accompanies him. Consequently, reflection and spiritual direction in the strictest form are required because the legion that kept him company over the years is not going to let go of him easily even though he has received the grace to discover sin and to find God. It is a case of extreme seriousness and we have to make the converted soul aware that severing its relationship with Satan is warfare that demands all of its attention.

After describing the roles evil forces play in our lives, I will now describe my personal narrative on the realm of evil. I could write an entire book relating to the workings of the devil in the world and in our lives to show souls what has been infused in my spirit. To be present before the tribunal of Our Lord is like an instant in the life of the soul in the material world. It is to discover the divine laws that reign over creation from which nobody can be exempt. To be outside the divine law is to be estranged from God, leaving us with two alternatives: eternal union or separation from God. The latter choice involves the soul undergoing the most horrendous suffering. To live apart from God is like the human body living without its soul; it is for all practical purposes in a state of death.

If we find ourselves separated from God because of sin, which is the presence of darkness that covers our souls from the light, we desperately search for Him until we find Him. Thus begins the state of purification of the soul that we call purgatory. The soul has to recover the light that was lost due to sin in order to perfectly unite itself with its Creator. I found myself in that state, separated from God and suffering profound despair at the prospect of not being able to unite myself with Him forever.

After showing me my life, the world, humanity, sin, heaven, I found myself unable to look at Him because of my own sinfulness. More than anything, I desired to bind myself to the good God, who is rich in mercy. However, I could not do this on my own because I was too intimately attached to the darkness through many years of sinful living in the flesh. I didn't even know if I should ask for mercy. The shame I felt was so intense that the possibility of being redeemed by the Lord escaped me; I felt separated forever. The spirit of evil made me believe that I would never be able to see Our Lord and that I would never reach heaven. I felt too unworthy to even think that I could return and see Him from the same inferno on which I was standing.

The Lord showed me a sin when I was 15 years old. That was in 1966 and I was witnessing it with my 47 year-old heart which made it even more painful. It seemed as though my adult heart was connected to that adolescent heart and was reliving the same scenario within the two different eras albeit with two starkly different perspectives. I found myself in the kitchen of a house in Bogotá in the company of a maid who seemed to be about my age. I knew what the Lord was showing me and knew perfectly well what the devil did to me to hurt this young girl. I had a macho attitude inherited from my ancestors and manifested it through my cruel, arrogant, superior, and abusive actions towards those whom I was supposed to have authority or dominion over. I spoke to her harshly, holding an object in my hand that she was supposed to have cleaned. She was staring at the floor and her face was flush with anguish. She neither protested nor showed a single gesture of resistance or disgust. On the contrary, the greatest act of humility and love was demonstrated on her part. My soul was torn apart when I saw this. She showed me that the Lord was present in one of the most delicate states of her spiritual and emotional life and my actions led her to a state of even greater suffering.

The act that I am describing seems very natural for us in our daily lives but the Lord called my attention to the consequences of how this fragile, humble and loving girl was placed in my life to either make or break it. She was the nobler one in the presence of the Lord. This hurtful sin in God's perfect justice was providing peace and love to this girl's family. It was turned into a grace, a blessing, in exchange for the suffering I caused her.

She had recently been separated from her parents, taken from the countryside where she was born and moved to the big city where she was placed in the service of strangers who had no love or charity towards her. Poverty, humility and love were meeting with harshness and spiritual ignorance, causing pain, anguish and despair. These types of acts are the ones that mark our state of emotions and the spiritual state of our neighbor, acts for which we are responsible before God. I learned the true sense of suffering by witnessing this painful sin. I understood how the evil spirits filled me with pride, vanity and pretentiousness. They attacked this girl because they knew her soul was with God and would receive these blows from the darkness without protesting or committing the minutest of sins, thus creating greater damage to my soul.

The worst damage that Satan can inflict is to provoke us to hurt a good soul because it is as though we are doing this directly to God. This does not mean that it is acceptable to harm an evil person, because that is in itself evil. The suffering of this child of God was a gift to her soul. I could see how her perfect act of love illuminated the spot where this took place. The demons that encouraged me to hurt this girl were not able to look at her because the light of God was resplendent in her. By reliving this sinful act, I was able to contemplate all the other sinful acts that centered on her during the few months that I stayed in that house. It was like seeing a sequence of events, all of them directed by the Master who knew one by one the consequences of every unloving instance. It was like observing a human being, mounted by a rider of darkness who uses our earthly life to injure the soul in the most terrible way, while at the same time causing great pain to all those we encounter in the course of our life. Only through the mercy of God do these painful acts turn into glory for the victim, revealing in this manner the true sense of the mystery of the cross, the mystery of suffering.

In the midst of this terrible scenario that seemed to last an eternity, I began to feel a great force piercing my being. It was at the moment when I was witnessing these horrible acts of cruelty on my part and feeling that I had sunk even deeper into the realm of evil that I discovered someone from heaven was interceding for my soul. As I explained earlier, I understood perfectly the origin, reason and sense of everything that I was going through since I was infused by the grace of the Holy Spirit and this was sufficient to understand everything without needing an explanation. I knew that help was coming from my guardian angel who interceded for me before the Lord and the Virgin Mary. This was reaching me through the love that my angel was presenting to the Lord. That same pure love was allowed by the Lord so that a continual flowing through the Virgin Mary could reach me, giving me the strength to be able to defend myself from such a great evil force that was dominating me through my guilt and shame.

This powerful force enabled me to stand up in the middle of this lake and gaze at the base of the golden rock that was touching the water. I didn't have the strength to look up to heaven but I was able to reach a piece of the rock that was the light of

God, which is hope and strength. I was attracted to the rock and when I looked at it the rock turned into bright, floating molecules. Piercing through it I fused myself with heaven and recovered the condition that I was in before I entered the sinful state. The Lord forgave me and separated me from sin and the territory of evil. I was filled with the greatest joy and an indescribable victory over the most horrific torments.

Suddenly, I found myself in the lake again surrounded by the territory of evil and facing a situation even more difficult that the previous one. To stand before the Lord's Holy Tribunal in mortal sin is the most appalling experience. Very few souls achieve salvation and most are relegated to a horrible purgatory. Some of them go to hell.

In order to more clearly understand the power of intercession, it is important to describe the action of the angels of God and the saints in our lives at the definite moment of our encounter with the Holy Tribunal. I briefly mentioned how evil forces act. Now I will communicate the action of all goodness coming from heaven that accompanies us through the grace of God. The trial that I will be referring to is a very short one. It was only a small teaching given by Our Lord so that I could be a witness to what awaits us according to the state of our souls. While it is hard to explain this experience, it seemed as though it was my real, definite judgment because the Lord always led me to believe that I was not returning to this earthly life and would be gone for good. If that had been so, I would not have been saved.

According to what I viewed in the presence of the Lord up to this moment, it was clear that my soul was condemned, notwithstanding all that was left to see. Only through the mercy of God am I here sharing this experience with you.

<u>Our Lives with God's Angels</u>

We have to begin by making it clear that these spiritual beings were created in heaven as pure spirits and had the freedom to choose their own destiny. They remained faithful to God during the rebellion of Lucifer and his followers. They become angels the moment they receive a mission on earth whereby they fulfill the will of God for man. The word angel signifies the action of a messenger, of executing a mission. The angelic spirits can be any of the nine choirs according to the mission assigned to them. The archangels, the seven spirits that stay in the presence of God, have been clearly represented with specific missions in the Old Testament and even in the New, continually acting until the Lord returns and reunites us with the New Jerusalem. We can see the actions of God's angels abundantly in Holy Scripture. Even in our modern times, we observed the angel of the Lord that came to Fatima in 1917 and announced to the three children the coming of Our Lady — the Virgin Mary. He taught them to pray and prepared them to kneel — prostrate — with face to the ground in the presence of such a celestial being.

From the very first moment that God instills life in a human creature and blows the wind of His Holy Spirit upon the soul, the Lord assigns to that soul a faithful guardian. Once life is conceived in the woman who will carry that baby, the battle begins with the enemy angel who will try to make sure that the soul never comes out of the womb. The faithful guardian angel begins the difficult task of defending the soul from the envious enemy. When the soul of the pregnant mother is in the state of grace, it remains strong and, in union with the mother's guardian angel, is a great spiritual protection for the innocent creature that is already being threatened by the forces of evil. When the mother's soul is in the state of mortal sin, the warfare of the mother's guardian angel is very difficult because that woman, though unaware, is supporting the mission of the evil one to destroy due to the fact that she is on his territory.

The angel of God supports himself in the blessings that the mother inherits through her intergenerational tree, as well as through the graces she might have received through the sacrament of matrimony had she been married in the church. In this case, the sacrament of matrimony, even though violated through sin, has an angel who is the guardian of that blessing. At that very moment, the angel is not shielding the mother but the child because of its precarious, innocent state. The guardian angel of the mother living in sin is limited by the relationship that she has with the devil who provides her with a fallen angel or a legion of angels who are guardians of her own destruction. When the sacrament of matrimony's guardian angel associates with the mother's guardian angel, the defense grows stronger. At the same time, the fallen angels are establishing a parallel attack using all the weapons that the mother and father of the child have given them by being in sin. It is obvious that the work of the devil in a pregnant woman due to fornication is to lead her not only to fornicate but also to murder through the lure of abortion. It is incredible what happens when we are in the devil's territory. He will give us a moment of pleasure in order to take away salvation for eternity.

In the case of a mother reaping the consequences of the sin of fornication but who chooses life for the creature gestating in her womb, a group of guardian angels will come to her aid that will protect her from the normal difficulties that the enemy will lay before her for having betrayed him. It is called treason because the objective of the evil one is to lead her to kill. If the mother repents and enters the grace of God, she will suffer great humiliations, discriminations and a series of difficulties that will represent before God a form of reparation because of the sin that was committed. If she does enter a state of grace, she will receive unconditional support from the angels anyway because she chose the life of the child but will retain the problems resulting from her maternity all the days of her life.

The angels of the Lord surround human beings because God in His infinite justice did not exile us to be destroyed by the enemy but instead provided us the opportunity of using the holy angels for protection. It is clear that humans determine the angelical presence in their lives — be it a fallen angel or an angel of God — according to their life of grace or sin.

We could say that from the moment of conception, a great reunion of angels (armies) welcomes us from both sides. These armies represent the total spiritual economy of a human being who begins the difficult path towards God. The final result of this exiled creature through his life in the flesh will affect future lives in a transcendental way. That is why a saint, upon achieving the highest level of purification, enters immediately to the same level as the angels of God and fuses with the Divine Essence to form the Body of Jesus, and in the process liberates many souls from purgatory through his purification. That makes it possible for future souls coming into the world and born into the flesh to receive the grace of God without having to face the army of the devil defenseless. For instance, the one who is born wrapped in darkness through the intergenerational tree of sin is without hope of spiritual armor because his ancestors wore it out through their transgressions. When our spiritual growth in the world begins, our relationship with the army of God begins and they guide all our actions.

When we are in the first stage of our life and have attained the age of reason, we establish a relationship with the angels of the Lord who guide all the areas of our human actions. We establish a direct relationship with the angels of our elementary school who guard all the areas of our youthful existence. When we are aware of the angels in our midst, we cannot at any moment think that they oblige us or dominate our decisions in any way. One of the things the angels of the Lord do is fulfill God's will. God gave us freedom to choose either the light that is guided and protected by the holy angels or the darkness that is guided and manipulated by the fallen angels.

If we live a grace-filled life, the holy angels become the greatest and most powerful companions we could ever imagine. They are present when we have decisions to make. Since they are in the light, they can see the final outcome of our decisions no matter how insignificant they may seem to us. Unlike humans, the angels possess full knowledge and can thus clearly see the effects of our actions. Being of pure intellect, they don't have to reason anything and instantly comprehend everything. They also possess the power of illuminating our intellect and imagination, guiding us along the path of holy creativity that edifies progressively a path of righteousness filled with work for salvation, placing ourselves in a territory of purification and reparation, providing maximum spiritual fulfillment in the period of grace of our life in the flesh, using our human existence as an instrument to reach heaven and occupy the place of a fallen angel.

Charity is one of the most powerful weapons against the devil. When we exercise charity with a truly humble heart, we are able to unite with an entire army of good angels. Every person with whom we are charitable to has a good angel and at that time all of them immediately unite themselves to us and form part of our defense and unconditional help. One who loves his neighbor has a charitable heart and is filled with celestial inspirations.

What we do in our childhood sets the stage for the rest of our life. It is then that we open a spiritual 'bank account' and begin to deposit the fruits of our deeds. Great battles have been fought during our childhood. Many lives are gravely altered at that age in spite of the action of the angels of the Lord because of the sinful lives of the parents. All areas of darkness to which the child is subjected are going to affect him or her in a negative way.

There is an enormous presence of the angels of the Lord in matters related to the economy because money is one of the greatest avenues used by the devil. Every instrument of survival is a means of battle between the two armies of good and evil. In the end, everything that we use for our sustenance is the fruit of one army or the other. If a person is found to be in mortal sin, most assuredly the devil ends up turning all his material possessions, including his own means of survival, into instruments of evil. His money will be administered by the forces of evil, enabling the devil to do great damage to humanity.

On the contrary, if one is in the state of grace with God, everything will be administered by the angels of the Lord, producing fruits of goodness with every cent. A financially-blessed human being who uses his money according to the will of God, like Lazarus (the good friend of Jesus), will be a precious instrument of heaven by which the angels glorify the Lord, performing great acts of love and charity that will shine more and more when presented before the Tribunal of the Lord.

A person who learns to master a given science that provides means of help to humanity and maintains his free will in the territory of the Lord will be used as a great instrument for the Kingdom of God on earth through the angels who inspire such knowledge. In contrast to this is a scientist such as Freud who achieved great scientific realizations but buried himself in darkness. By validating human sexuality as a means of expression to liberate humanity from all the emotional repressions emanating from the maternal womb, he inflicted on humanity two of the greatest crimes: abortion and homosexuality. The justification of a promiscuous lifestyle freed man from his moral code, consequently debasing him to his animal nature. The saddest part is that this teaching has a true scientific component that has been falsely applied. The theory has a real base but in practice it has become twisted and perverted.

A human living in God's territory is offered a sure solution to every human dilemma that presents itself. His thoughts, intentions and actions are guided by the light that elevates everything to a level of perfection because they are in absolute harmony with his spiritual growth towards God. At the same time, they open up an accessible path to everyone around them, generating a sea of light in union with light itself, which is radiated by the great numbers of God's angels who surround the creature in the state of grace.

The longer a person continues to be in the state of grace, the greater light that is assimilated because the presence of angels and saints increases more and more, turning the person into a real fountain of light. It is a continuous fight to maintain the light of the divine spirit, which is like a lamp that shines over every step of this earthly path to heaven. When we walk in the darkness of sin, we erase these instances of grace and our soul absorbs obscurity (darkness), producing anguish, insecurity, anxiety and depression.

The return to the light after we have strayed from the true path and fallen into darkness is tremendous because we can see the tracks that were left behind on the enemy's territory. It is costly to clean our soul and to recover our innocence, light and angelic company. The same light enveloping us allows us to clearly see that the best way to cleanse ourselves is to do so immediately; otherwise, it will be more difficult.

These are all automatic reactions that generate a return to grace, particularly the acknowledgement that it is in the flesh that we have to cleanse the garment that has been soiled by sin. Once we are stripped of the flesh, it is impossible to repair what we have damaged. If the mould is defective so will its accompanying product. We have to correct the mould before we pour the product in it — in this case, our soul. We have to take into account that every good inspiration is fostered by the angel of the Lord and has divine inspiration as its essence. The angel of the Lord is a messenger of grace; therefore, everything the angel activates in us is the product of Divine Will. Neither angels or saints or human creatures are outside God's will.

The Lord's angels have a hard time guarding the deposit of consented temptations accumulated by humans while in exile on earth. Every temptation comes to us through the senses that develop into passions or are introduced by passive thoughts that lie dormant. By abusing food or alcohol as a result of relaxing our spiritual guards, the same demons who brought those goods and excesses to us accumulate and store them, patiently waiting for the consented idea that doesn't come from the light to materialize. The angels of God guard that given deposit making sure that it will not be executed, constantly promoting an inner cleansing through confession, fasting, penance and mortification. These weapons help us to maintain the cleanliness of our souls, which are unceasingly being bombarded by proposals that tempt us each day. That is why it is said that even the most just man is able to sin seven times a day, this obviously being a theological conception.

Spiritual maintenance is difficult to master and the most important battle to conquer. Our souls depend on it in order that consented sins do not accumulate and turn into currents of darkness that can break loose and get out of control. After living in the grace of God for many years, many people allow the accumulation of a great number of consented temptations to enter their souls. We can see them totally drowning in a decadent world, far removed from grace. There are a lot of priests, religious and consecrated laity in this category who become trapped in the most abominable sins after having lived an exemplary life filled with work for the kingdom of God. The spirit of evil presents a brilliant argument of justification to the devotee who had previously been out of his clutches, making him believe that he needs to relax from such discipline since he is only human and falling will make him stronger when he has to get up again. There are millions of tactics used by the enemy to ensure that the soul that falls into the darkness remains there, where he can pervert it more and more. For this reason, the person who doesn't rise immediately after falling will have difficulty finding the strength to do so later. The longer it takes for him to recover, the more likely his return path will be fraught with danger.

The soul that most appeals to the devil is that of a priest, religious or consecrated layperson because bringing them down violates the sacred tabernacle of Our Lord. A great sacrilege is committed as if the spirit of evil has entered the tabernacle itself. By giving his life to the Lord, the consecrated soul is turned into a tabernacle of God. The angels of the Lord erect great fortresses of the celestial militia around human creatures but always respect their freedom. Nothing that comes from God obligates or dominates.

Inviting our guardian angel to accompany every action of our lives is a holy procedure that helps us to intimidate the devil who tries to ensnare us. The manifestations of love and loyalty with which we are gifted by our association with our angels, feed and strengthen us, like the water that soaks the plants. The Lord has assigned each of us a guardian angel during our earthly life that associates with many other angels in order to provide maximum support for the soul that the angel is protecting. The entrance of a soul in the state of grace before the Tribunal of the Lord is like the triumphal entrance of a soldier returning from war escorted by a great army of warriors who kept him company during battle. It is the triumph of the soul, the day of the crowning of the Christian. On the other hand, the entrance of a soul filled with sin before the Tribunal of the Lord is like the arrival of a prisoner surrounded by his jailers and in the company of the most saddened celestial guardians who were rejected by the soul. This is a painful march, a lost battle, the conquering of evil. Only Divine Mercy can change such a terrible imprisonment of the soul in the territory of the evil one.

It would be necessary to write a whole treatise to elaborate on the role in our lives of God's angels who never cease to teach and guide us. I believe I have been able to describe briefly their function, giving the reader a glimpse of what I have learned from these holy spirits of the Lord.

The Saints: Their Presence and Actions in Our Lives

The saints' spirits, although in the company of angels, weren't created pure but were purified in exile in the material world through the life in the flesh. This constitutes one of the greatest miracles of creation and is the greatest testimony to the mercy of God.

Sanctity on the human plane is comparable to the act of loyalty that St. Michael demonstrated when the angels rebelled. One becomes a saint by perfecting a pure act of loyalty to the Creator, while rebuking everything that comes from darkness during one's lifetime. The triumph of the saint is the crown of the Christian, the holy envy of the angels of God.

Our Almighty Father forgave our original sin and gave us his Son as our new Adam to renew through Him the eternal paradise from which we were thrown into exile. God created a soul from the very vessel of clay from which one cohabits the flesh, turning it into a pure spirit that occupies the space that was left empty by a fallen angel. The concert of souls that flow from the Creator towards the earth and from the material world towards the Creator constitute the divine cycle in relationship with the New Jerusalem — the second coming of Jesus. The spaces left empty by the fallen angels will be filled by the saints to complete the salvific plan of restoring paradise. St. Paul states in the First Letter to the Corinthians (6:3): "The saints will judge the angels."

Saints are the most intrinsic work of the Creator. The mystery involves the purification of man through the flesh. In the beginning of creation, the angels — being of pure intellect — were able to see in an instant the plan of creation and some of them rejected the idea of serving a man who, created as an inferior creature, was able to grow to an angelic level. Those many disobedient angels produced the great following of Lucifer. Their rebellion resulted in their subsequent condemnation and expulsion from heaven. In retaliation, they turned against God's creation — man and the loyal angels.

God, whose ways are higher than ours, uses the devil's ire to contribute to the purification of the saints. Despite all of Satan's snares that he inflicts on humanity, the saints still manage to stay focused on God and remain loyal to Him. The persistence of the devil in propagating evil makes it all the more probable that God will allow it because through these flagellations God molds His creatures of clay and purifies their souls so that when they are set free they can finally embrace God forever.

A human creature that walks on the path of sanctity finds that a very clear spiritual world begins to present itself in a beautiful form as he draws closer to the divine light. God does not allow a soul to suffer any torments imposed by evil forces that it is incapable of resisting or enduring. The path of sanctity is the pure reflection of the crucifixion and resurrection; in other words, it is a route that leads one to a painful death but triumphs afterwards, with Jesus turning tribulation in the flesh into a ladder that leads to heaven.

The vivid presence of the Holy Spirit in the life of the saint illuminates the eyes of the spirit, presenting the spiritual battle with absolute clarity. This makes the saint's journey through life even more difficult but he is able to find strength by fixing his eyes on the path to the celestial kingdom that is already visible. A human creature, having received the grace of sanctity from God, achieves the strictest spiritual direction. If a saint occupies the place of a fallen angel, then that explains their ferocious battle not to be replaced. The celestial army, by divine design and through the action of the messenger angels, is in charge of fighting the ongoing battles being waged shoulder to shoulder with the saint here on earth in order to help him achieve celestial glory.

The Lord has prepared many mansions for us and that is why we observe how the history of sanctity has left us with a rich legacy of spirituality inspired by different angelical choirs based on divine designs on the chosen souls; to put it simply, every saint may be guided by a plethora of angelical choirs based on the grace granted to him by our Almighty Father. With this knowledge in our hearts, we are able to comprehend why the saints merit our devotion and can appreciate the power of their intercession. The saints do not need to carry their graces from this life to heaven because heaven is pure grace; therefore, all the graces of the saints accrue to us for our benefit here in exile — given to us through the intercession of the Lord.

When a priest prepares himself to celebrate the Holy Eucharist he dresses up in the sacred garments appropriate to the liturgy. His garments cover up the sins of the flesh in order for him to more worthily approach the altar of sacrifice. By the same token, when praying to the Lord through the intercession of a saint, we are dressing ourselves up in a garment fit for this saint in order to cover up our sinful flesh and to present ourselves to the Lord, making supplication to His mercy as a pure act of humility. A saint's intercession before Our Lord is comparable to a situation in which a younger brother in the large family is looking for support from an older brother who is on good terms with his father to obtain a certain necessity. Both are petitions and acts of humility, one involving the human family and the other the family of the Lord.

We know that a middleman is not needed when we go to God because He is a good God who is merciful and will always listen to us with love, but the act of intercession is even greater before the Lord because it covers us in humility like the man in the gospel — the publican — who was invoking the Lord from the gate of the temple, not daring to get close to the foot of the altar.

In the midst of all the beauty that the reality of spiritual sanctity had to offer, I saw with clarity the obstacles that the monks who rebelled against the Church had faced because of the envy that the devil had planted in their hearts. When they found that the path to heaven was the way of the cross: suffering, sacrifice and severe spiritual discipline, they chose to separate themselves from the universal Church in order to put together a new plan of salvation that highlighted the forgiveness of sins and the grace of Pentecost. That way, one did not have to face the cruel, painful reality, which was Calvary or carrying the cross with Our Lord.

We are called to be like Christ and to live His passion; by not allowing the flesh to die with Jesus, we are only celebrating the resurrection. In order to spread the seeds of dissent, they deserted the guidelines of the Church founded by Our Lord and continued in an endless race to divide the Church.

Just as the prodigal son spent his fortune and had to seek forgiveness from his father, they went to a foreign country to spend Our Lord Jesus Christ's treasure and one day would have to return home repentant, begging forgiveness of Mother Church for having squandered the means of salvation. I am speaking here about our separated brethren who founded Protestantism. It is sad but, nevertheless, allowed by Our Lord who in His infinite love also forgave the Apostles when they denied and deserted Him during the most important time of His passion.

The saints in heaven intercede for our souls at the moment we present ourselves before the Holy Tribunal. It is there that we discover the result of all our prayers. The communion of saints extends during our lives here on earth according to the fruits of past generations who prayed and were loyal to the Lord. They also obtain blessings for many future generations, so much so that even ignorant sinners who are far from God receive the benefits accumulated by the spiritual battles of our ancestors.

There are saints who by divine design perform angelical duties by relaying messages pertaining to salvation assistance to the chosen souls, thereby uniting themselves with the celestial hosts who permanently extend their hands to help souls attain salvation and manifest themselves in a very personal way to these souls. At the same time, the chosen souls receive the grace to understand the mystical language of the messenger saint who brings weapons for his spiritual battle. There are countless ways of leading souls to heaven, which can be summed up by explaining to the reader that everything heaven gives us comes with the assurance that it is going to be manifested to us with clarity. I am sure that many of you can identify with this because you have experienced this grace, which is difficult to explain in human terms.

The saints intercede for the souls who are in a state of purification in purgatory, especially those who have shown devotion to them. Many of these souls need to resolve pending matters concerning their earthly life. These souls have come to the realization that the severity of their suffering is linked to the state of their soul at the time of death. While such souls are undergoing suffering in purgatory, the saints continue to intercede on their behalf to make amends for the sins that were not atoned for on earth. As well, they will use all their good deeds to lessen the time of their purification as a result of their bad deeds.

We know that the souls in purgatory are no longer able to repair the damage in the flesh caused by sin. We also know that everything could be healed and set free in Jesus Christ, Our Lord; therefore, the soul has the opportunity to leave the state of purification through the intercession of others over everything that has not been repaired in order to fuse with the divine grace of heaven. This proves the infinite mercy of God towards His children who followed the path of salvation but were unable to reach the final destination of perfection during their lives in the flesh.

In the gospels, Christ exhorts us to be perfect as His Heavenly Father is perfect. He shows us the path, the way, the truth. He promises us eternal life but also warns us that it is better to resolve our accounts with our brothers in this life because if we do not do so, we will be taken to jail and will not be able to leave until we have paid the very last cent. I do not think that there is a better example or a clearer description of purgatory than the message given by Our Lord in this parable of the gospel. He demonstrates in every possible way that the only path to salvation is sanctity; therefore, let's not wait or expect that living a Christian life — accepting Jesus as our Savior, reading these words and proclaiming them everywhere — is enough to obtain perfection and reparation of our sins. We must also embrace the cross with acts of authentic sacrifice and legitimate charity, living every day more and more in the purity of faith and obeying the Ten Commandments without a doubt. In doing so, we display our loyalty to God and, in the process, become more like Him.

The saint supports every loyal action of the human creature but is very strict, as is our guardian angel. He will not tolerate iniquity being the motive of prayer intentions. When the penitent does not fulfill the promises and walks in spiritual disloyalty to accommodate what is material, the saint speaks sternly to him and departs. The saint is loyal to man when man is loyal to his devotion. The only way in which a saint is able to intercede for us before Our Lord is if the penitent is able to present himself at the foot of the Lord with a humble, contrite heart, recognizing his nothingness, his misery and imploring mercy from the Holy Tribunals. Only a soul such as this will be able to gain the intercession of a saint. We cannot fool a saint or Our Lord.

The communion of saints is fully active and intertwined in our trinitarian reality of the church: the triumphant church in heaven, the suffering church in purgatory, and the militant church on earth. This 'holy trinity' unites itself with the Holy Trinity of Father, Son and Holy Spirit to establish the Kingdom of God — a most-powerful union.

The lives of the saints parallel the lives of sinners but the saints go directly to heaven and the others to a painful purgatory or eternal damnation. The saints transform themselves into true lanterns of light in wells of living water. The flow from the Creator to His creatures turns into healing and deliverance for those who cross their paths or receive their benediction because they carry in them the living Christ who renews souls; these souls help Him carry His cross. The moment a saint acquires the crown of the Christian soldier in the glory of Our Lord, he undresses himself from the flesh and establishes his presence over purified territory on earth in a spiritual purity equal to the angels. Through the legacy of good works left behind on earth, he continues the battle for souls until the day of Our Lord Jesus Christ's return. It is clear that the mercy of God is truly grand during our exile. We are indeed blessed to have a celestial family to assist us in this valley of tears in meriting the gift of eternal salvation.

Continuation of My Own Trial

The spiritual presence of sin before the Holy Tribunal is the greatest pain a soul could ever suffer. Every sin is an absence of love, meaning the absence of divine perfection; the greater the sin, the greater the absence will be, creating in the soul a void so large that it would be absolutely indescribable in human terms. This pain is unspeakable and beyond compare. To be before divine perfection presents instantaneously an absolute truth; all the darkness that sin has brought upon the soul turns into the greatest obstacle between the creature and his Creator. The soul that rebukes all the darkness of life in that encounter only wants to fuse itself with the true fountain of love.

I found myself in a territorial evil so grave that I had lost all hope of seeing the light of the Lord. I had just been forgiven of a very serious sin only to find myself in a much worse sin. The feeling was as though I was totally covered with the most horrible, rotten wounds but I could not see them and was unaware of their horrifying smell until suddenly, to my astonishment, they began to appear one by one, stirring in me the most profound sadness.

The more we confront the reality of sin, the more we accept our misery, our nothingness, and our voluntary separation from God. That perfect state of conscience first illuminates evil in our souls using the element of surprise and horror to reveal the gravity of our evil acts and partnership with the devil. Whatever little strength was accumulated spiritually during our earthly life hangs at the balance. However, this may be offset by the prayers of those people conscious of the soul's needs that come to our assistance and present their supplications before the Lord.

The strength that is received through any intercession coming from the light is enormous, no matter how small it is. Even the smallest acts of love are capable of radiating over the soul potent fuels of spiritual strength and hope. I was clearly able to see all the aspects of the light that were supporting me at the precise state of sin in which I was found. The enemy is not able to face light. Every act of love gives the soul the power to recreate itself, even mine in the midst of such desperation. Loving acts will also defeat a lot of darkness and allow the soul to gain some strength in order to guide the heart over the shame towards the fountain of love that is absorbing the soul eternally. I was standing on evil territory and, in spite of this, my soul was not done in yet. I found myself in the final battle between eternal life and death.

"At the hour of my death, call me. From the evil enemy defend me." This is a powerful prayer. If we only knew the power God has given us through prayer; if we only knew the glory awaiting us; if we would only be loyal to God and spend our lives on our knees asking Him to allow us to be purified through the strictest penances during our lives in the flesh. But the flesh can turn into our worst enemy and it speaks to us from the clay from which it originates. The world traps us in such a way that we are encouraged to think that anything alleviating suffering or pain is a triumph; on the contrary, it is a curse. The evil one augments the fixing of our human eyes on a materialistic life where the pleasing of the senses, instincts and reason are the only focal points of life's journey, turning us into slaves of our own passions and instincts.

I found myself surrounded by the most vicious and degenerate fallen angels that one could ever imagine. I knew that the image I was about to face before the Lord was going to be a horrifying scene. I was placed in the very act of it at age 21 in Hamburg, Germany. I saw a big room where I was rehearsing a play with a German actress who was also 21 years of age. It was a play with a lot of sexuality. Both of us were the principal actors. We decided that it was better to execute the sexual act in order to give a sense of reality and intimacy to the play. It was only an intellectual justification guided by lust and stimulated by the evil spirits who had planted in us that seed which we pleasantly accepted.

I will never be able to explain the pain I felt when reliving such a scene before heaven. We turned into a single body and it seemed as though we would never be able to separate ourselves from one another. We appeared with four legs, four eyes and four hands. It was a macabre scene that only pushed me further away from the presence of God. Understandably, I was totally convinced that I deserved to stay forever in the darkness, in the midst of the most horrifying eternal separation from God and in the hands of the most monstrous enemies. The inclination of the soul before such a dark situation is to accept its misery and separation from God because of the shame magnified by the presence of the enemies of the soul.

The spirits supporting sexual impurity are so horrendous that we can recognize immediately that the more impurity we accept from them through temptations in our lives, the more we end up acting like them in the flesh. By witnessing them move around that scenery of sin, I was able to see how they had trapped me in it, how they had sold our flesh to one another, how they had intensified the fire of our passions to allow them to be fused, thereby turning us into a dirty unit and separating us from the possibility of ever looking at or facing the light.

I noticed how I had taken on their mannerisms and gestures. I was given special talents to cultivate the opposite sex and made weak so as to be captivated with ease by women through carnal passion. I recognized the work done by the enemy when he gave me infernal gifts in order to seduce others without effort and to be seduced even more easily. When we find ourselves in evil territory, the type of evil spirit that is guiding us influences our behavior. In some cases many spirits or an entire legion participate. I could clearly see at that moment that it was a combination of the spirit enemies who long before had seduced me and the ones who had seduced her early on in her life.

A perfect power from hell snares us unceasingly. We lead a life of impurity, permanently depriving ourselves of grace during our earthly journey. This, in turn, keeps us from feeding our souls, takes us to the lowest grade of spiritual poverty so that when we find ourselves before the Holy Tribunal, we will not have an ounce of strength to face divine light; therefore we will have no alternative but to accept darkness as our only outcome. Today, the spirit of impurity manipulates many people; I observe them flaunting the mannerisms of the devil who breathes through their eyes and through every gesture of their bodies by every word they pronounce and by the way they laugh. This is a sad and cruel reality.

The impure spirits make us believe that to capture an awakening sexuality is a normal and permanent part of human existence. This stance intellectually justifies passions of the flesh as private property that should be fed in the same way as a beast is fed in the circus — being thrown live prey so that it can be savored in its hot blood. In the same way, man, too, maintains his ferocity and his wild state is kept alive and palpitating, fanning the infernal circles enkindled during his journey on earth. I could see all this — that was me in all possible aspects of sexual impurity; all the demons that were after me due to the impurity of my ancestors was like fuel that was permanently ignited — the fire of my own sins. In the midst of such a horrible separation from God, divine intercession gave me the strength to overcome that sin and fuse myself with the light of the Creator but again I weakened and fell into another state of impurity even greater.

Intercession is so extraordinary that it is indescribable, not to mention the greatest gift of Divine Mercy. Every time a sin of mine came before the Holy Tribunal, especially a particular scene, its effects were mitigated due to the intercession received from heaven. It is like saying that every wound of sin possesses a particular organism of infection and should be healed according to its state of decomposition. While being tempted to commit sins of the flesh such as the one I mentioned in particular, I witnessed the presence of many angels who had been engaged in the battle against the enemy. Included were my guardian angel and the guardian angel of the person or persons who were companions of such temptation. They made great efforts to dispel it and while they had the power to stop us, our sinful act took away their capacity to protect us. At the very moment of witnessing our weaknesses, the angels implored God to give them the opportunity to deliver us from the horrible encounter about to take place. They were interceding for us while we were deciding to sin. I want to remind the reader that I am describing myself — a soul who came before the Holy Tribunal in a state of mortal sin for 33 years.

As an example of the different forms of intercession involved in combating impurity, I'm going to present to you a scene that I related in the beginning of this story with Donna and Cindy. Both relationships were a 'gift' from the very same group of evil spirits who had led me from my early teens with all the elements that were going to captivate me. They were associated with all the evil spirits who were already keeping me company, plus the ones who were keeping company with these two women. We found ourselves in the midst of an unimaginable spiritual battle because in this case another group of evil spirits joined in, bringing gigantic corruption to our generation through the hippie revolution. If only Our Lord would allow you, the reader, to observe for an instant what I had witnessed before His Holy Tribunal in reference to what the arrival of these two women represented in my life and vice versa, it would be an immense warning as to the seriousness of the battle being fought for our souls. I was able to perceive the importance of our lives as if a symphony of souls in concert. Our destiny is eternal life in heaven but we are constantly being invaded by the cruelest enemy whose goal is to torment us for all eternity in hell.

My relationship with Donna was the beginning of the longest sequence of infernal events in my life. Through her, two different venoms were injected in me: one of hallucinating drugs and the other of promiscuity. The latter was given to me through intergenerational inheritance and throughout my short journey of impurity until the moment of my teens. Donna brought a fire of impurity that ignited and never ceased to extinguish itself until I found the Lord at age 47.

It is not necessary to narrate all these sick, impure sexual acts in the way they were presented before the Lord because by describing the consummation of the first impure act, the reader will have a clear idea of what occurs in relation to impurity of the flesh. What is necessary is to convey the different strategies employed by the evil one. In order to prepare me for the coming of Cindy, he would establish a fount of corruption using his tools of darkness for the many people whom I would come into contact with. Cindy and I were the cause of a lot of souls being destroyed; through us, they were initiated into LSD and a spontaneous, relaxed sexual life.

Writing this is painful. The evil one enlists us in his army and prepares us to lead great movements of impurity. This entails meticulous preparation on his part beginning in our youth, which gradually lasts a lifetime. The evil one knows the gifts and talents that the Lord has given us and he wants to snatch all these capacities to his territory early on in our lives, otherwise they will become weapons that will be used against him.

Both women were physically beautiful and very intelligent. They were shrewd and fast, coming from an industrialized metropolis — a world that was out of reach to us in Bogotá. At that time in the 1960's, Bogotá was a relatively small city and one with a provincial atmosphere where the simple lifestyle of the inhabitants accounted for their ignorance of urban life. These two apparent ambassadors of heaven came from a place where life was lived on a mundane level and the two of them reunited all the necessary elements to completely enchant me.

Up to that time I had never met any woman so young who possessed the astuteness and worldly knowledge these girls did, much less their level of liberation. I am by no means declaring myself a victim of these two girls. On the contrary, the mixture that Satan concocted with the three of us had all the necessary ingredients to intoxicate a whole crowd. I am only describing the side that belonged to them. I supported them in each one of the intentions that was leading us to the abyss, helping them to fall further and further down without having the faintest idea that it was truly the result of evil since it was taking place in the midst of the most beautiful friendship. I am neither stating here that we were the puppets of Satan, nor that we didn't have the power of decision because, if anything, we were conscious that we were doing something against everything that was addressed in the moral law of God.

It is an indescribable and incomprehensible mystery how God allows the enemy's snares to strip us, leaving us undressed in our virtues. I believe this is the most opportune moment to obtain Divine Mercy because we can be lifted up from the bottom of the abyss and shown the true path of love from which we were led astray. After being rescued by the Lord, we become true soldiers of His army with full consciousness of the weapons of evil that were used against us and instantly able to recognize them in the future, enabling us to stand firm in the army of the light. Using everything we learned from our struggle with the devil, we are now able to assist in the righteous battle to liberate captive souls. In other words, our experiences with the devil can contribute to the salvation of souls if we teach others the same lessons we learned. Unfortunately, there will always be the mysterious exception of eternal perdition of so many souls who never reach the Creator and are left damned, wailing in the darkness. Who can explain this? Only God can.

I will not be able to find out about the numerous evil spirits who worked for the perdition of my soul as well as Donna's and Cindy's, and for the fall of so many other souls who I hope were not wasted eternally, until I finally face the Lord before His Tribunal. This evil army presented a great battle of which will be very difficult to explain the final outcome until the moment of Divine Mercy.

Our own heavenly army, as much as the army of God that keeps company with every person we meet, enters into an immense and immediate battle against evil in order to save us. During the many months that Cindy and I were together, in the midst of our most intense activity, some of the angels of God, sadly enough, were in a position where they had to fight against us in many instances. In retrospect, I can see the urgency of Satan using our youth and vitality to keep us active without rest day and night; to us at the time, it appeared to be the most extraordinary life of love and pleasure, something never dreamt possible.

Satan knows how short and transitory our earthly life is. He knows he has to use the vital moments of our existence to exact the greatest damage so that when we reach a mature age, we no longer have the strength to change, even if we so desire with all our hearts. He fortifies the idea of believing in this world and centers our concentration on earthly life so that when we do so, he, in turn, can expel the light out of our souls. This is a typical case of souls taking the wrong path and expunging Christ from the center of their lives after being graced at birth by the sacrament of baptism. Only the mercy of God can save us then. God only knows the path by which the devil took us away and only He can send His angels to bring us home, gradually showing us the way back. By taking the journey towards hell and back, we are able to recognize the evil ways so that we never again return to the path of iniquity that only serve to steer us into great spiritual darkness.

Life in the flesh can lead us down the road to perdition or elevate us to eternal happiness. Sometimes, at the death of a good, young person, we wonder whether he was freed from the hands of the devil by Divine Mercy because God knew the plans of the dark one that were to be wreaked against that particular soul and took it away for salvation sake.

Cindy was led to a great abyss and ended up dying of a heroin overdose. As previously mentioned, the evil one used me for many more years, taking advantage of my vitality and artistic inclination. There is no talent that attracts Lucifer more than the arts. Through manipulating the arts and the artists, he has captivated millions of souls throughout the world especially during this period of human history. The evil one rapidly develops such talent to the highest levels because he nears the very end of the end times.

Today, more than ever before, we see an ever-increasing number of young stars climb the artistic stage, cloaking themselves in man's power, wealth and fame. Their high profile and influence provides them the platform to potentially corrupt millions of souls as the masses strive to emulate the decadent and worldly behavior of these stars. Every artistic talent that I possessed was used by the evil one to increase the venomous influence of my actions.

My experimentation with drugs began when I became acquainted with Donna. We smoked marijuana and later I graduated to LSD, mescaline, PCP, hallucinating mushrooms and many more types of drugs with Cindy. From the very beginning Satan led us into drug trafficking because anyone using drugs eventually ends up trafficking. Once you begin to use them, you want everyone else to do the same; eventually, you end up buying them for everybody. When you buy drugs for other people, you end up getting your own personal portion free of charge. Such elicit drugs demand an income that you do not possess. Your life turns into a life of promiscuity — a very degenerate life. What goes on after this cannot be described because we all know there is no good end to such a path of darkness.

The evil one uses these addictions to lead individuals into the most despicable, impure and perverted actions. The outcome is a jail sentence, tragic death or horrible disease, not discounting exile from the community, loss of reputation and identity. All this encompasses the strategy of hell — the gradual way of taking the soul down — popular in the latter days of the end times.

The sins of impurity carried out during that period with Donna and Cindy, as well as all the women with whom I had sexual relationships with before the time I married at age 20, were presented before the Lord as a group of events that together culminated in one single circumstance. They were led by a legion of evil spirits who arrived from North America with my friends from California and another legion that accompanied me from my hometown to Bogotá. It is not possible to describe, much less write about, the way in which I faced this before the Holy Tribunal. The best way to explain it would be to take the first scene of sexual impurity by narrating it so you know that every illicit union in the flesh not only binds two people as one flesh but permanently unites them with the territory of evil unless they clean up their ways while in the flesh by freeing their souls from the chains of impurity through conversion. Every one of these sins will be present before the Lord's Tribunal and the perpetrators will have to go through each one of these impure sexual acts, painfully face them, and be subjected to the most horrific persecution from the evil one who will make sure that each scene is relived and that its consequences penetrate the recesses of the soul. The soul that is oppressed by such sins falls into a bottomless pit, separated from God. Again, I tell you, only by the mercy of God can a soul be saved from the grip of its own sin.

Until the time I was 21 years old, I lived a spiritually miserable life. No one could imagine what I witnessed in my vision. A group of evil spirits, all linked together one after the other, put together every single relationship that I had. Each one of them established themselves sequentially and seemed to come casually but in reality, everything was planned. The devil knew who was coming next to continue the bankruptcy of my soul and the souls who would be corrupted through my actions. That would mark hundreds of people in the future who would each be impregnated with the venom of promiscuity. This is like a cancer that gradually invades the cells until it is interrelated with the whole organism, which in this case is humanity.

We can ask ourselves: Where were the angels of the Lord during this time? What were they doing? Why did the Lord allow such evil, such impurity? The answer is written in the gospel. God does not oblige His creatures; He gives us the freedom to choose and decide. Without exception, every person who was involved with me as I walked along the entire path of impurity — regardless of how young they were — did what they did by their own free will, accepting all the proposals that were presented by the spirits of evil and teaming up with them to propagate evil. Our guardian angels, as mentioned earlier, never leave us but only turn into sad witnesses when we are walking in sin, as I was.

All the guardian angels of those who were with me during these years in that fiery circle of impurity were part of an immense battle trying to reduce the impact of the evil one that was intent on hurting each one of the souls. But it was a limited battle; only the blessings inherited through my ancestors and the few acts of devotion that may have been made at an early age were giving the angels of God strength because the territory of that particular presence was contaminated by my own conscience. There was nothing the guardian angels could do except intercede for my conversion.

I feel it is important to present to the reader another territory of sin that brings about transcendental consequences: the tongue. Jesus taught us that what hurts man is not what comes into his mouth but what comes out of his heart. He told us with perfect clarity about the consequences of the tongue. If we want to know who really lives within us, listen to the words that come out of our mouths. By the same token, if we want to find out whom we are dealing with, all we have to do is carefully listen to the words that come out of their mouths. It is painful to discover when standing before the Lord's Tribunal that every word that comes out of our mouths becomes reality and is recognized before the presence of the Lord. It is also quite an eye-opener because the majority of human beings do not pay attention to what they say and what they hear. Nevertheless, words that have our consent become part of the same deed whether spoken or heard so we should always discern what we say and hear because both may convict us. The spoken word is such a powerful weapon. When we pronounce the name of Jesus reverently, all knees bend; however, when it is used to curse, everything withers. The apostle James gave us a teaching on the tongue that should be read frequently.

One of the many acts that the Lord presented to me in the area of evil related to my tongue. It became a weapon to commit a terrible offense against a schoolmate in elementary school who was being teased by the other students. The worst nickname he received was the one I gave him. He carried this nickname throughout his life and had to endure humiliation and persecution from everyone, which caused him great anguish. This boy grew up suffering from isolation and extreme loneliness, which conversely purified his soul in a precious way that no one can imagine. His purification caused enormous damage to the souls of all those who contributed to his holiness. This may appear confusing but it is exactly the way it took place before the Lord. If we do not pay attention to the cruel acts that we commit against helpless and innocent people, we will undergo great spiritual consequences.

One could argue that I was too young to know better and did not have a fully formed conscience because I was only in elementary school at the time. On the contrary, this is only a rationalization because wisdom appears before the Holy Tribunal of Our Lord, wisdom that rings in the soul at the moment of birth and precludes us from feigning ignorance to justify committing such an act. The soul feels the pain of sin at the very moment the sin is being committed or even consented to in one's mind. Therefore, there is no excuse.

I learned that every single sin that has not been confessed and atoned for is guarded by demons. To explain how this operates in our spiritual economy,

I am going to provide you with a particular scene that I faced before the Lord.

A group of people lined up in front of a bank teller early one morning. For some reason, the teller was working very slowly. One of the people in the lineup became restless and started to complain, cursing the bank, its employees and then the government. The people in the lineup became agitated and began to grumble too, so that when they eventually met the teller face-to-face, they also insulted him. Consequently, the teller lost his temper and behaved badly for the rest of the day. The chain of events that developed in the bank spread to other parts of the city, causing a rise in hostility and violence, and then across the ocean through the telephone, generating an incredibly-high radius of evil actions. By the end of the day, acts of extreme violence were being committed as a consequence of one person's reaction to a teller not working quickly enough.

When we present ourselves before the Lord's Tribunal, we will be responsible not only for our direct actions such as those that occurred in the lineup before the teller, but also the end result of the chain we started to link together earlier by our impatience.

The evil one knows the final outcome of our words because, unlike us, he does not live in limited time and space. He can instantly maneuver the tongue of his disciple to ignite a horrifying fire.

It may sound exaggerated, but I am nonetheless going to share with you what is, in all likelihood, the most recent example of an incident that I can recall from my spiritual experience before the Lord. I'm not going to give you the worst scenario because I'm not pretending to write a book about spiritual terrorism. I know that only by this particular example will the eyes of the soul see what needs to be set straight thus far before it is too late.

How many times does a person curse a son, brother or friend, saying horrible things, robbing them of hope and peace? How many times has a person been wounded for the rest of his life because of a great verbal assault spewing forth from a loved one's mouth? The terrible onslaught occurred because the person speaking the abusive words was unable to control the selection of words coming out of his mouth. Those verbal darts were inspired by the evil one who knew exactly the type and strength of venom to shoot at that particular moment to create the greatest injury — a wound aimed at piercing the person to whom it was guided, hurting the perpetrator as well. I am referring here to the sinner who is not in the state of grace with God and whose tongue is in the hands of the enemy.

The tongue is a relatively small organ that can perform either good or evil acts. Gossiping is one of humanity's cruelest deeds. It is probably one of the weapons that cause the greatest damage to the soul, especially to the gossiper's soul. Even though it may appear at least to our earthly way of thinking that the victim of gossip is the one affected by it, the truth — spiritually speaking — is that the reverse actually happens. The gossiper is the one that ends up being hurt, whereas the victim of gossip has an opportunity to purify his own soul.

Besides being used to create false testimonies, gossip can also serve to reveal the truth about others, knowing that its effects can be detrimental. Sometimes the devil is so astute that he entices us to share a certain secret concerning someone. We are led to believe that we are doing them a favor by communicating the evil that we appear to notice in them. The truth is that this pretense on the part of Satan of helping is one of the subtle, little traps in which most people fall. A spirit of division that causes conflict generally inspires people who are overly protective towards us. That is not to say that having a protective inclination is evil; however, there is something amiss in the drive that leads people to be overly protective. In such instances, we are better off telling these people not to love us so much.

Just as the tongue shapes the course of our salvation, so too does the will which, if not in conformity with God's, can lead us — body and soul — to hell. Every malicious individual savors the moment, and even experiences a burning in his heart, when the venom injected into his words purposely strikes the intended target causing damage. The pain of witnessing this act before the Holy Tribunal is so immense that it cannot be described in words. Let it suffice to say that each word coming out of our mouths is either a 'deposit' towards our salvation or a 'withdrawal' towards our perdition.

When the Holy Spirit guides our tongue, it is in God's hands. As we experience this state of grace, everything that emanates from our mouths is filled with love and serves only to purify, strengthen, support and forgive. Our speech enlightens, inspires and presents a permanent sense of hope. When the tongue is in the hands of the devil, that particular tongue curses, corrupts, lies, accuses, judges, torments, complains, is unforgiving, impatient, contaminating, vulgar and malicious. To be aware of the administration of our soul's economy is the most important calling of our relationship with God. No one from the earthly life will be with us to lend support before the Holy Tribunal. We alone are responsible for our own behavior — good or bad. Our actions will be our only witnesses at the judgment.

Some human beings make regular use of obscene language in their everyday speech. They use rationalizations to justify it, saying it's part of the culture and accepted by others around them. Thus, their tongues become instruments of entertainment and pleasure. Such individuals are puppets of the devil. Satan uses the tongue to try to corrupt the atmosphere and chase away any angels of God who may be surrounding those who are in God's grace. I realize that speaking of angels that surround us might appear ridiculous to those stuck in the reeds, unaware of the spiritual combat going on around them.

The truth is that we are all surrounded by good or evil whether we believe it or not. Anyone can provide reasons why God, purgatory or hell does not exist but this will not change the truth. Most assuredly, they exist as my earlier witness testifies. The Lord asked me about the great talents He gave me — the Catholic faith. Given the talents that are given to us, we will not be judged before the Lord based on our religion, race, nationality, or any other beliefs, but on how we loved God and our neighbor. The Lord explained to me that it is easier for a pagan with no knowledge of Christ or the Creator who is leading a life in harmony with God, his neighbor and himself, to find salvation than the Christian who had the appropriate tools of knowledge, doctrine, religious orientation, etc. at his disposal and chose instead not to use them, burying them the way I did.

As I stood before the Lord's Holy Tribunal, He settled the question as to why I had been standing on evil territory. The Catholic Church was a blessing bestowed upon me. It was a product of many generations in an alliance with each other, going as far back as Abraham. To have been born a Catholic was neither an accident of human destiny nor a simple decision made by my biological parents. They did not impose this on me. The Lord brought this reality to my attention when He showed a flashback of me abandoning the Church when I was 14 years old, leaving behind the sacraments that were protecting me in this material world. The contamination that I went through in the 1960's (which I have already explained in detail) led me to forfeiting my God-given talents. Consequently, I was left unarmed, just like the pagans who lack specific guidance on their life's journey. My habitat naturally became one of ever-increasing darkness since I had no resistance to evil forces.

The enemy knew only too well my blessings and that the mystical presence of the Church in me had to be replaced with another spirit. Everyone born with the blessing of Christianity receives in baptism the fire of the Holy Spirit, which nourishes life in the flesh. That is why the devil replaced it with oriental paganism, occultism and all other kinds of esoteric practices, creating an apparent 'life in the spirit' that gave me the illusion of being within the wings of the Holy Spirit.

I rejected the talents the Lord had given me and led others to do the same. Besides making fun of those talents, I put forth the most absurd arguments to demonstrate how unnecessary it was to be part of the Church, thereby belittling Christians, especially Catholics. The Lord showed me that He came to earth in bodily form to repair the damage in the flesh due to sin — past, present and future. He left us with a sacred instrument in the flesh represented by the priest. Having received the anointing of the priesthood, they are able to free us from sin and the chains that bind us to the devil.

When our Lord told the apostle Peter that He was giving him the keys to the kingdom of heaven and that whatever he would bind on earth would be bound in heaven and whatever he would loose on earth would be loosed in heaven, He instituted the Sacrament of Reconciliation. This sacrament turns the priest into a spiritual vessel of the Holy Spirit. The Lord explained to me that when we are with the priest in the confessional, we should pray to the Holy Spirit so that the priest's physical presence disappears and is replaced by the Holy Spirit during our confession. The priest in his humanity experiences the same misery of the penitent — sometimes even more so — because his life is consecrated to the Lord. This makes him a double sinner if he commits a sin. That is why the life of a priest and his allegiance to God should not concern us. It is strictly a personal relationship between the priest and the Lord.

The power of the Sacrament of Reconciliation is tremendous but often underestimated. Used to its full potential, it will guide us into solving one of the heaviest burdens that we carry — a burden we should unload before presenting ourselves before the Lord. I highly recommend the practice of this sacrament. When we decide to confess our sins, we inadvertently arrest all the activities of the devil in our lives. We in effect take him captive before the Holy Spirit and hand him over with his entire army to the confessional where he belongs. If our hearts are repentant, the Holy Spirit will at long last release us from the grip of the evil one. Should we die after making a sincere confession, we will be present before the Holy Tribunal of the Lord, standing in the territory of goodness, unlike in my particular case where I was facing the Lord with my feet planted on the devil's territory.

Although we can be sure that our sins are forgiven through confession, reparation does not necessarily result from simply confessing our sins. The perfect act of reparation begins with the Eucharist. Since Jesus Christ became flesh in order to repair in His flesh the damage due to sin, what better flesh is there for this purpose than the very same Body and

Blood of Jesus Christ in the Holy Eucharist? Coincident with the washing away of sin by confession is the cleansing of our spiritual house, which should immediately be occupied by the Lord so that the enemy cannot take up residence through a spiritual vacuum. If we truly believe that Jesus dwells in the Eucharist where His Body and Blood is in the form of bread, then our act of reparation will be consummated, leading us to make atonement for our sins. However, not fully believing in the real presence will make our act of reparation imperfect. If we happen to present ourselves before the Lord at that moment, our souls will still be stained with sin. We must purge ourselves of this stain of sin but if we are no longer in the flesh, this vessel of clay that committed these particular sins can only repair them in the state called purgatory.

In this case, we will not be standing in the territory of evil because our sins have been forgiven but it will be necessary to be perfectly clean before entering eternal paradise. One of the best ways of repairing ourselves after being forgiven is to try not to sin again. Nonetheless, when it inevitably happens we must immediately go to confession and repent before sin begins to destroy our souls again. If we stay in mortal sin longer than a day we will enter into the excrement pit of the devil and end up in worse condition than we were before we last went to confession because the devil strikes more ferociously at those who have fallen.

Catholics generally question the logic of going to confession frequently because they expect to commit the same sins again. The reason for frequent confession is very simple. How do we know the Lord will not call us tonight? One of the cleverest tricks of Satan is to make us believe that confessing our sins directly to Jesus will suffice and that there is no need of a middleman. If that were the case, what would have been the role of the twelve Apostles chosen by Christ to go out and proclaim the Good News of salvation? The Lord could have done this without the Apostles — the middlemen. He could have been spared the frailties of the human body and the incredible agony of His passion and death. When the Lord paired His disciples and sent them out, they were given the power to forgive or retain sins. He told them, "Those sins that you forgive will be forgiven and those that you retain will be retained." How could one dispute this command by Jesus? The Sacrament of Confession was undoubtedly established at that time.

Jesus uses our flesh to bring about positive results; it is through the flesh that we are redeemed. By pouring His Holy Spirit over us, everything that sin has damaged is purified and we become Christ-like — images of Christ. It is no longer a mystery how the prophets, seers and priests are used as instruments of God. For example, in the Old Testament, we can comprehend why David didn't kill King Saul in the cave. It is because he was aware of the anointing that God gave him. God manifests Himself through His creation and we are His most treasured creatures. So important are we to Him that He gave His own Son to bring His lost sheep back to the fold. Satan's trap is to entice Catholics to focus on the sins of the Church in order to weaken their faith until they become his slaves. If we fix our eyes on Jesus, we will be saved but if we concentrate on the sins of the priests, nuns, or any believer for that matter, we will never be able to detect the presence of God in our Church or any other church.

People born into the Catholic Church who stubbornly persist in focusing on its errors and join the Protestant church will not be judged as members of the Protestant church but as cradle Catholics who had left the Church. God will not judge us on the basis of the churches to which we belonged but if we have been stiff-necked in our interactions with our brothers and sisters, He will severely punish us. Those born into the Protestant church will be judged as Protestants since that was the talent they received from the Lord. There is no reason for a Christian to lure another Christian from a different denomination away from his church on the grounds that Christ is more present in one church than the other.

This is enough reason that something is very wrong. We are not called to convert our fellow Christians, only those people who don't know the Lord. It is like entering the house of a married man and trying to convince him that his marriage is not good enough and offering to find him a better spouse. This is the sad reality of many Protestants whose mission is to draw Catholics away from the Catholic Church. Some Catholics also feel compelled to lead Protestants to Catholicism. As Christians, we all belong to Christ; therefore, we should stay where the Lord has called us unless God provides the Protestant with the grace of embracing the Catholic faith in which case it will be the gift of a greater duty and responsibility within Christianity elevating his spirituality. Let us turn our separate lives in Christ into a family unit, even if we worship Him under different roofs.

The Lord introduced me to the treasures of a 2000-year-old church — the Catholic Church, which has been following Jesus' footsteps all this time. The sacraments of the Church are so powerful that if they were performed with reverence, motivated by love of God, they would conquer a gigantic portion of the devil's territory. The Lord also showed me how Satan enters the Church through those who are in sin, creating the most incredible state of confusion and spiritual disarray for those weak and lukewarm in the faith that have not firmly decided on which of the two spiritual territories they reside.

According to the Lord, the Church is plagued with a record high number of disloyal clergy in this day and age. Fortunately, there are loyal priests and religious, referred to as the remnant, who maintain some balance in the midst of this darkness. Our Lord promised that the devil would never prevail against the Church. The dogmatic and liturgical configuration of the Church is mystically formed by divine inspiration as a sure-fire weapon to defeat the enemy of the children of God. The Church gives glory to God and, at the same time, is an instrument of salvation for human beings in their earthly exile; its divinity serves as a refuge, even while standing on the burning coals of an inferno on earth.

Divine issues are hierarchical. For many Christians hierarchy begins with the local parish. When we are aware of the significance of our parish, we enlist ourselves in a battalion. Every soul should report daily to its battalion. Everything we do, every prayer we say and every intention of the heart that is directed towards God should be presented before the tabernacle of the parish. To be united in the spiritual battle of our parish is to be automatically united with the trinitarian church: the militant church on earth, the triumphant church in heaven and the suffering church in purgatory.

The strength that a real soldier of God acquires in the Militant Church is so overpowering that the evil ones will run away from him. That is why it is important to discern where we are in relation to this trinity of churches. In which hierarchy do we circulate? He who exits the hierarchy of light immediately enters the hierarchy of darkness. No place exists without a hierarchy. We are either on the side of good or evil. A group of criminals do not approach someone who is protected by bodyguards; by the same token, the devil and his army will not confront a Christian who is wearing the uniform of a loyal soldier whose strength comes from being part of the army of God.

That is why it is important to understand that when we enter our Church, the Lord is there to greet us. We cannot anchor our faith in the humanness of the Church. If we could only fathom the beauty of the spiritual life in our Church during the celebration of the Eucharist, a visit to the Blessed Sacrament, the Stations of the Cross and any devotions performed within the Church, we would visualize the sacred nourishment that our souls are filled with in the temple as we look for the Kingdom of Light while living through this, our exile. That is our Church, our refuge.

<u>Mercy</u>

Our loving actions performed while on earth are the most powerful sources of light. To illustrate this, I will tell you about an act of love during my childhood while I was attending elementary school at the age of eight. During recess, I was sitting on a wooden bench on the main patio of the school beside a child who was physically deformed. By the grace of God, I became his protector during breaks between classes. Many of the children were making fun of him and abusing him when the Lord inspired me to embrace and protect this helpless, abused child. During my personal judgment, even though I was in the enemy's territory, I witnessed Divine Justice.

During the time the Lord was showing me the child's embrace, my sins that were appearing before Him were not being taken into account. It seemed as though these acts of love towards this child had turned into a single one before the Holy Tribunal, representing a grace that was erasing territorial sin by leaps and bounds. I could see every single wrong that approached the Holy Tribunal and watched it disappear in the presence of the Lord. If I could describe it in human terms, I would say that love and charity is the currency of heaven.

In order to acquire the Kingdom of Eternal Life, a soul standing before the Lord needs only to possess the love that has been given, shared and propagated during life, as well as the love of suffering. Love is the divine essence; thus, it is from this particular element that we receive true nourishment of the soul.

Charity is one of the most powerful tools we can use to sow the seeds of love for the salvation of our souls. This act of Divine Mercy towards a soul that is lost (such as was mine) teaches us a lesson about the spiritual wealth surrounding us in this material world where the true eternal treasure is only visible to those souls who walk in the light and discern the true values of the spirit. All the treasures of heaven that are at our daily disposal will produce the greatest pain if we don't recognize their worth while we have the vehicle of the flesh to capitalize on them spiritually. Love, charity, forgiveness, compassion, patience, tolerance and all other holy virtues are the deposits that will protect us from bankruptcy of the spirit. They will build up our eternal wealth in the celestial bank.

We spend most of our lives passing up golden opportunities for enriching ourselves with real treasures because we are too concerned with accumulating material ones which will eventually become dilapidated, if not stolen beforehand, by thieves. The perfect act of reparation is centered on love. Everything that has been wasted as a consequence of spiritual ignorance caused by sin can be recovered with charity. The same act of reparation can be solidified with a firm purpose of amendment whereby the heart, mind and soul are united in a spiritual battle centered on defeating sin, assuring the promotion of grace at every instance, in every place and under any circumstance.

The soul walking loyally with God acquires the knowledge of His mercy and benefits the most from it. God's mercy is inexhaustible and He wants to reassure the soul of His desire for their freedom from every attachment to sin so that when it leaves the flesh, it will be spiritually rich.

Economy of the Soul

At the moment of conception, the soul begins an accounting, a spiritual accounting where the calculations commence and are added to the total sum of the spiritual economy of his biological family. This is called intergenerational inheritance. If the biological mother is not in God's grace and in intergenerational debt by inheriting all her ancestors' debts, in other words, under the yoke of original sin, her baby will begin a difficult journey, facing adversity every step of the way that will conflict with his spiritual expectations of goodness. These expectations exist because of the soul's inherent state of grace before leaving the mother's womb and entering sinful territory.

Baptism frees the creature from all intergenerational debt, as I have already explained, and the soul's economy enters a field of grace where the Divine Judge opens a brand new account.

When we begin to sin, the freedom gained through the Holy Spirit by baptism is lost and our spiritual economy hangs in the balance. After baptism, every soul has an unlimited spiritual potential. The soul is like a treasure chest, being filled with jewels of goodness that will undoubtedly lead to spiritual enrichment and harmony with the material world. Every spiritual treasure is an asset to the material world.

A soul whose spiritual economy is no longer tied to intergenerational debts and attachments is an anointed being, blessed by the Holy Spirit. God pours oceans of abundant grace over the faithful soul.

The subject of the soul's economy is an extensive one that requires in-depth analysis and explanation. I will elaborate on this topic in another book.

The Holy Virgin Mary

Everything is created in Jesus. Each time I was before the presence of the Lord He would assimilate into heaven surrounded by angels and saints; He would turn into Divine Justice in His infinite mercy. Our Lady, the Virgin Mary, appeared filled with grace. The same way Jesus fused himself with His creation allowing me to see that everything was in Him, so Mary unveiled all the graces she was holding.

In one of these splendid moments when Jesus was transformed into heaven and Our Lady appeared to me, the aching, every-present void in my heart due to the lack of love I had received in my life, disappeared. The only truly pure, maternal love that can fill the womb of the spirit is the love of our heavenly Mother because it is perfect.

Because of original sin and human nature, man is prone to feelings of inner conflict concerning his biological mother. The most common reaction of a son who is confused and trapped in the face of life's difficult circumstances is to confront his mother, asking why she brought him into the world. Subconsciously, we blame our earthly mothers for the hard-hitting reality of being born to die. When we place the will of our lives entirely in God's hands, we begin to understand the mystery of eternal life and gradually are able to accept our mortality. Then we are replenished with heaven's graces and, in turn, find sustenance in the new Adam and Eve — Jesus and Mary — who are immortal, the fountain of pure love and the gateway to paradise.

My encounter with our heavenly Mother was the greatest gift I could have received, especially in light of my separation from her during all my earthly existence. Experiencing Mary's love during our earthly journey fills us with indescribable inner strength. As well, the security of having a mother who will listen to our cries of anguish, ease our sufferings and help us bear our trials and tribulations is a great blessing. It is sad not to know Mary as the Queen of Heaven and acknowledge her as not only the mother of Jesus but also our mother, for the journey in this valley of tears is very difficult without her. It is even sadder to be sons and daughters of such a powerful Queen and not accept her in our hearts, refusing the graces that she so willingly desires to grant her children. By allowing her to be the Queen of our hearts, we also allow the man-God to enter into us — the One who metaphorically turned into a cross in her womb. She carries in her womb Calvary, Golgotha, the crucifixion and death of her Son and the cross itself. Above all, in her Immaculate Heart, we find the victory of the resurrection and the triumph over Satan. Mary is the hope of the saints.

It is necessary to be on the path to sanctity in order to embrace the Queen of Heaven in the human heart. We have to focus on the way of the cross through her eyes because she was the faithful witness of the heartrending torture and death of her Son. She had to deliver her Son to the hands of violence. She was by His side the entire time He was trampled, spat upon, humiliated, despised and beaten on His way to Calvary. She stayed with Jesus to the bitter end at the foot of the cross; that is why that particular cross is alive in her womb and her heart.

As I mentioned at the beginning of this testimony, I was united with Mary by a spiritual umbilical cord. Everything that I was receiving from heaven went through her first. Similarly, everything that emerged from my heart and moved towards heaven passed through her. Could there possibly be a more perfect gate to heaven and Jesus than the Holy Virgin Mary? Mary played such a vital role in my mystical experience and made it so meaningful that I must dedicate a whole account exclusively about her to do justice to what I have been through. I pray that the Lord will give me the opportunity to write an extensive version of my encounter with Our Lady, the Virgin Mary.

Conclusion

Sometime during the fourth month of my kidnapping ordeal, after I had given the rebels everything I could muster (though much less than the amount of money they were seeking), I was informed that they were awaiting instructions for my execution. For the next two months, I lived anticipating death at any moment. The manner of death would be the only surprise element. Thus, whenever I saw one of the criminals cleaning a machine gun, I thought I would be shot. If someone walked by with a rope, I figured I would be hung. If a knife was being sharpened, I imagined being stabbed. If we were in the vicinity of steep mountain slopes, I awaited being thrown down an abyss. Thoughts of death continuously permeated my daily existence. On at least two occasions each day, I experienced what I interpreted as my final moments of life.

One day, at 2:00 a.m. in the morning, in the midst of torrential rain, I was untied from the tree that I had been shackled to and ordered to follow four of the criminals. From that moment on, through the early hours of the morning and the rest of that long, weary day, they led me through one of Columbia's western rainforests — a mountainous, dark and forbidding jungle. Later that evening, after the sun had emitted its last rays, we approached a dark, unpaved road. The four men ordered me to walk straight ahead without looking back. I approached with dread what appeared to be my final moments on this earth. As my legs felt paralyzed, I set forth with difficulty — each new step being a burdensome weight as I awaited the ominous sound of a rifle piercing the silent night. I begged God to let me be shot in the head so that I would be killed instantly rather than being mortally wounded and left to suffer an agonizing death alone on a lonely, secluded road. I walked and waited, walked and waited, but nothing happened. By now, I had gone a very long stretch. What was up?

Approaching a curve in the road, I mustered the courage to shift ever so slightly my gaze backwards. A totally unexpected sight greeted me. The men climbed back up the mountain in the direction of the woods from which we had come! I quickened my pace. Dare I hope? I was free for the moment but how long would it last? Would I be intercepted by another group further down the road and taken into captivity again? My heart beat rapidly as I scanned the horizon for signs of humanity, but no one appeared.

About half an hour later, an old bus miraculously appeared, stopping just a few meters ahead of me to unload what was clearly a female guerrilla. As she went her way, I quickly walked towards the door of the bus. It closed in my face. I pried it open, entered and walked all the way to the rear where I found a bench on which to sit. At that very moment, reality pierced my soul in a glorious way. I was a free man. God had covered me with His most infinite mercy, giving me a second chance at life. The terrible nightmare was finally over.

After a few days of physical and emotional recuperation, I went to a Discalced Franciscan monastery in the city of Pereira, Columbia. There, Our Lord placed me in the hands of a holy Italian priest who introduced himself as José Maria de las Cinco Llagas (Fr. Joseph, Mary of the Five Wounds). His name filled me with indescribable peace, as did his words of absolution after patiently hearing my lengthy confession sometime later. What a blessed day! What profound joy I experienced — the heavy burden of years of accumulated grievous sin lifted from my weary soul...forgiven and free at last — thanks to the mercy of God.

I spent over a year reliving my mystical experience silently within myself — speaking only to the Lord about it. Mistakenly, I thought it was our special secret. But such was not the case. He manifested Himself to me during Holy Week in Bogotá, Columbia, showing me that everything He had infused in my heart through the mystical experience which took place during my captivity was to be shared and to become my new mission in life. He waited for my reply. It was with great difficulty that I gave my consent to the Lord — not because I didn't want to do it, but because I felt so unworthy due to both my sordid past and lack of understanding as to how I was to relate such mysteries and mystical experience. Moreover, how could a sinner like myself witness to the people of God around the globe, sharing what I had seen, heard and been commissioned to do by Him? Of course, I did not know that the Holy Spirit would be my constant guide and teacher at this early stage in my spiritual formation. This realization would come later. I now understand that without the Holy Spirit's assistance, I would have nothing to discuss. The only request of me was to be faithful, to pray, to read the Word of God and to give my testimony later. God promised to express Himself through natural means, using my own language, symbols and speaking style.

To date, I have given witness in many countries. I have trusted in the Lord's promise and allowed Him to fashion the topics and words and select the locations and recipients of His messages. Thus, the preparation of every talk has been left to Him. I will continue the mission to which He entrusted me as long as He wills it, despite any obstacles (health, spiritual combat, etc.) that may present themselves.

The topics I have touched upon in this book (through my particular testimony) are limitless in scope. The knowledge of divine theology is an endless gift greater than creation itself. All the angels, souls and creatures living in the territory of life exist in an eternal flight towards the infinite fountain of the Creator. Thus, the journey towards God never ends. His knowledge fills the soul with an infinite grace, joy and thirst. To be possessed with a love of God by a spiritual hunger that has the capacity to become more sublime with time, greater than anything worldly — the soul desiring God and increasing union with Him. What a great blessing it is to be loyal to God who is infinitely good and merciful. Should this not be our greatest consolation? God, our loyal, lifelong support, desires to resurrect us from sin so that we may experience to our maximum capacity the wonders He has prepared for us in the Kingdom of Light. Accordingly, He invites each of His beloved children to walk with a healthy spiritual economy, in complete honesty before the Divine Judge, His Son, Our Lord Jesus Christ.

I testify that the Lord is alive in the Holy Trinity of the Father, Son and Holy Spirit, active in our lives and always ready to rescue our souls from exile, to elevate us to His heavenly kingdom. Christ's mercy is infinite. He forgives our sins and His kingdom will have no end. I also testify that the devil exists. An angelic creature who fell from grace, he is the enemy of our soul, the king of an infernal, futureless hierarchy, who tirelessly lies waiting, ready to do anything in his power to snatch both sleepy and zealous souls for his kingdom — a kingdom void of any joy or peace. At the same time, I testify that Jesus has already defeated him and that this enemy of our soul will have no power over any of us who believe in Jesus Christ as our savior and redeemer. However, he who lives in mortal sin (as I did at the moment I was presented before the Lord) is a slave of the devil and is in imminent danger of condemnation. I testify that I have been rescued from the darkness and will never trade the treasures of this world for the real treasure — Jesus — that I have found and carry in my heart. I will continue to testify with my life and witness to the world wherever the Lord leads me until the day He calls me before His presence again. I ask the Holy Spirit, who led me to write this book, to bless those who read it with love and an open heart. I ask Him to restore their soul's economy in order to be a witness to the light and inherit the kingdom that is already in their midst and given to them so they can testify that Jesus is their King and their Lord.

May the Lord bless you always, dear readers. May the Lord preserve you in the light, have mercy on you and yours and allow you to be a fruitful apostle of His kingdom, sharing with everyone that Jesus Christ is Lord.

Printed in Great Britain
by Amazon

42202359R00118